The Tot Shabbat Handbook

The Tot Shabbat Handbook

A Practical Guide for Engaging Young Families in Congregational Life

Edited by Paula Feldstein
with a foreword by Eric H. Yoffie

URJ Press
New York, New York

This publication was made possible by donors who wish to remain anonymous.
Their gift was inspired by their granddaughters, who showed them
that Reform early childhood education was the first step
toward a lifelong commitment to Reform Judaism.

Lbrary of Congress Cataloging-in-Publication Data

Feldstein, Paula.
  Tot Shabbat handbook / Paula Feldstein.—1st ed.
      p. cm.
  Includes bibliographical references.
  ISBN 978-0-8074-1141-4
  1. Sabbath—Study and teaching. 2. Preschool children. I. Title.
  BM685.F455 2010
  296.4'1—dc22
                              2009030173

Printed on acid-free paper
Copyright © 2010 by URJ Press
Manufactured in the United States of America
10 9 8 7 6 5 4 3 2 1

Contents

Foreword

*Train a child in the way he should go, and even
when he is old, he will not depart from it.*

Proverbs 22:6

Shabbat, the centerpiece of Jewish life and the most joyous of our celebratory days, is among the greatest gifts we can give our children. Indeed, over the years, Tot Shabbat in our congregations has become a time that is beloved by all who help young families bring Shabbat into their homes and into their lives. The blessings, the food, the music, the candlelight, and the rituals all create an ambiance that transports us—no matter our own age—from our fast-paced, hectic daily living to a welcome place of meaning and holiness.

As you—rabbis, cantors, teachers, lay leaders, and parents—strive to train your community's youngest children, instilling in them a love of Torah and Jewish living that will stay with them all of their days, we are pleased to offer *The Tot Shabbat Handbook*. In addition to a useful collection of creative ways for young families to celebrate the queen of days, its pages are filled with Tot Shabbat basics that address the philosophy behind the program and include developmentally appropriate teaching practices, music, sample programs, and hands-on how-tos for sharing the joy of Shabbat with a roomful of young children and their parents.

May this guide give you tools, ideas, and enthusiasm with which to share the gift of Shabbat with the youngest children in your family, in your congregation, and in your community, and together may you experience Shabbat joy, Shabbat holiness, and Shabbat peace.

Rabbi Eric H. Yoffie
President, Union for Reform Judaism

Preface

When I was a rabbinical student at Hebrew Union College–Jewish Institute of Religion twenty years ago, no one was talking about Tot Shabbat. The students weren't talking about it, and neither were the faculty. However, I was fortunate that my husband, Rabbi Jordan Millstein, had an internship with Rabbi Elyse Frishman, who was at the Reform Temple of Suffern (New York) at the time. Rabbi Frishman had a monthly Tot Shabbat at her congregation, and she quickly taught my husband, and through him she taught me, how to lead a Tot Shabbat service. But Rabbi Frishman not only taught us how to lead Tot Shabbat, she taught us why Tot Shabbat was so important and how it was real worship and needed to be treated as such. As we entered the rabbinate, this knowledge and commitment to young families went with us to the congregations we served. Over the years, my Tot Shabbat services have evolved and changed somewhat, but what is still clear is the fact that Tot Shabbat is an important worship experience for the families who participate. While I have changed some of the songs and added new ideas, the core of my Tot Shabbat service remains the same. Tot Shabbat is a worship service for young children (pre-readers) and their families. It is not story time (although a story might be told in the "sermon" slot). It is not playtime (although there should be a lot of movement and fun). It is not time for parents to schmooze (although they definitely should have schmooze time at the *Oneg Shabbat* afterwards).

Tot Shabbat is worship that is developmentally appropriate and spiritually meaningful for young children and their families. It is a time for young children and their families to pray, sing, and connect with God and their community. It can be a very powerful and important experience for both the children and adults present. While the content of a Tot Shabbat must be appropriate for young children, it should not be so boiled down and infantilized that the adults present find it meaningless. On the contrary, one of the challenges of Tot Shabbat is to make it effective with young children and speak to the adults as well.

A few years ago, I realized that there were many of us doing Tot Shabbat all over the country, yet there were no resource materials to help us or the congregations yet to begin their own Tot Shabbat worship. Only if we were lucky enough to learn from someone else (as I was) did we have a clue how to conduct a Tot Shabbat. It seemed obvious that we needed a resource guide. The goals of this guide would be twofold: to help those who had never done Tot Shabbat before get started, and to provide new ideas to those of us who had been doing it for years. I approached Rabbi Hara Person at URJ Press and found out that she and others at the Union for Reform Judaism had also been thinking about the need for such a book. All we needed, of course, was a donor to make the project happen. Recently, we were blessed with a donor who also recognized the need for such a resource in the Reform Movement. With the vision and guidance of Rabbi Eric Yoffie, Rabbi Jan Katzew, Rabbi Sue Ann Wasserman, Rabbi Hara Person, Nancy Bossov, and Cathy Rolland, the project began to take shape.

As we worked on the book, we began to ask an important question: Would a Tot Shabbat resource book be complete without a CD of music? Music is clearly such an important part of any worship, and especially of Tot Shabbat. A CD of Tot Shabbat music would definitely be the icing on the cake. Under the leadership of Cantor Elaine Katzew, Steve Brodsky, and a wonderful committee of musicians and Tot Shabbat leaders, a CD has been produced. We hope that it, with the book, will be a great resource for all Tot Shabbat leaders, both the veterans and the beginners.

Working on this book has been a true labor of love. I have met, reconnected with, and corresponded with so many amazing people who are doing such incredibly creative work. Our conversations have been thoughtful and inspiring. Even though I have been doing Tot Shabbat for almost twenty years now, I have learned so much from those who have contributed to this book. Those who lead Tot Shabbat know its power and put their hearts and souls into their work. To all of you who helped with this book, in large ways and small, I am incredibly grateful. To all of those at the URJ who had the faith in my ability to produce this book, I am so thankful for your support. I am also grateful to all the congregations and their staffs who enthusiastically responded to my requests for their outlines, photographs, and ideas. However, I would be remiss if I did not especially thank Cathy Rolland, director of early childhood education at the URJ, who has been there every step of the way with ideas, support, enthusiasm, and solutions to every problem. I also feel a debt of gratitude to Michael Goldberg, who stepped into Rabbi Hara Person's shoes (big ones to fill) and has patiently led me through this process. Last, but certainly not least, my heart is full of gratitude to my life-partner and best friend, Rabbi Jordan Millstein, who supports me and inspires me every day with his love for me, our family, the Jewish people, and God. Our two daughters, Eve and Sarah, remind me over and over that nurturing the Judaism and spirituality of our children is one of the greatest ways we can serve God.

To all of you who lead and support Tot Shabbat in your synagogues, always remember that you are engaging in holy work and making an incredible impact on the Jewish lives of our families and the future leadership of our congregations. We hope that our offerings of words and music will help all of you who engage in this holy task.

Rabbi Paula Feldstein

Part I

Why Tot Shabbat?

Never Too Young to Pray

Sue Ann Wasserman

Praying is like humming.
Worship is like being part of a choir.

Humming comes instinctively, naturally to us. We often hear young children humming their own tunes as they play by themselves.

Being part of a choir is very different. There are many skills we must learn in order to be a choir member. We need to learn to control our breath so that we can support our singing. We need to become skilled at reading musical notation so that we can learn the pieces. We need to learn how to listen to the other voices in the choir so that we can blend in with them—creating a beautiful sound.

Praying comes instinctively, naturally to us, especially when we are young. If that openness to faith is nurtured from our earliest years, it is more likely that we will develop a lifelong relationship with God.

Worship is very different. There are many skills we must learn in order to feel comfortable praying with a community. We need to learn to read Hebrew so that we can recite the prayers. We need to learn a wide variety of melodies so that we can sing with the congregation. We need to learn the choreography of worship—when to stand, bow, sit—so that we can move together with the community.

Tot Shabbat worship is a priceless opportunity to nurture the innate prayerfulness of our youngest congregants, for whom ". . . spiritual thoughts and feelings are as much a part of the growth process. . . as their physical, mental, or emotional development."[1] The Tot Shabbat setting is the perfect opportunity to encourage children to ask questions about faith and God—to teach them how to uncover who God is for them. Yet prayer is not just about us and God: "Prayer encourages an awareness of the world around us. It makes us pay attention when we are otherwise preoccupied."[2] It's never too early to help children focus outward to the world around them—to teach them about helping others, being kind, and taking care of the earth.

Young children, unlike most adults, are open to a wide spectrum of ways of praying: singing, speaking, storytelling, drama, movement (dancing, marching, clapping, and so on), sitting in different places (on the bimah, on the floor, in a parent's lap), and art projects (not in the sanctuary, of course) to name just a few. Tot Shabbat worship shouldn't look like adult worship. It needs to be engaging and age appropriate. But also remember that it is the first step in teaching children worship and prayer skills that they can build upon. So while you will use a variety of approaches to prayer, it is still important to develop a repeating, recognizable order to the worship, to use some prayers and melodies that are part of your congregational worship, and to teach about the sanctuary as a very special room—different from other rooms in which children spend time.

Tot Shabbat can be as important a worship experience for the parents who attend with their children. Since worship isn't a "spectator sport," parents should be engaged throughout. They are their children's most significant role models in everything—praying included. Yet we know that many of our parents weren't raised with strong Jewish backgrounds, so the Tot Shabbat setting should be a safe place for them to gain knowledge and prayer skills as well. The Tot Shabbat leader should model for parents how to talk with their children about God.

Tot Shabbat isn't all about prayer. It's also about creating a place for parents to meet other parents who, like them, are just beginning to raise Jewish families. Helping these families connect with each other will strengthen their sense of being part of the synagogue community.

Most importantly, perhaps, the Tot Shabbat experience is an opportunity to encourage young parents to begin developing their own family Shabbat and religious observances. The impact of regular Shabbat celebration on the Jewish identity of children is significant. In his December 2007 presidential sermon at the Sixty-ninth General Assembly of the Union for Reform Judaism, Rabbi Eric Yoffie called on Reform Jews to take Shabbat seriously and to begin to define for themselves a regular pattern of Shabbat observance:

> In our 24/7 culture, the boundary between work time and leisure time has been swept away, and the results are devastating. Do we really want to live in a world where we make love in half the time and cook every meal in the microwave? When work expands to fill all our evenings and weekends, everything suffers, including our health. But families take the worst hit. The average parent spends twice as long dealing with e-mail as playing with his children.
>
> For our stressed-out, sleep-deprived families, the Torah's mandate to rest looks relevant and sensible. Our tradition does not instruct us to stop working altogether on Shabbat; after all, it takes a certain amount of effort to study, pray, and go to synagogue. But we are asked to abstain from the work that we do to earn a living, and instead to reflect, to enjoy, and to take a stroll through the neighborhood. We are asked to put aside those BlackBerrys and stop gathering information, just as the ancient Israelites stopped gathering wood. We are asked to stop running around long enough to see what God is doing.
>
> And this most of all: In synagogue and at home, we are asked to give our kids, our spouse, and our friends the undivided attention that they did not get from us the rest of the week. On Shabbat we speak to our children of their hopes and dreams. We show them that we value them for who they are and

not for the grades they get or the prizes they win. During the week we pursue our goals; on Shabbat we learn simply to be.

All of these are a part of the Tot Shabbat experience: cultivating regular Shabbat observance, creating community, providing a safe worship experience, teaching worship skills, modeling God-talk between parents and children, and fostering a love of Judaism and the synagogue. (Did you think it was just a chance to tell a story and sing a few songs?) So plan this synagogue experience as carefully as you would an adult worship service or a class in the religious school. Draw on the resources you find in this book and within your own congregation; experiment and ask for feedback from participants. But most of all, share your love of prayer, God, and Judaism with those you lead during Tot Shabbat.

Notes

1. Katy Abel, "Children's Development of Spirituality," Pearson Education, Inc. For the full article, see http://life.familyeducation.com/spirituality/religion/36537.html.
2. Rabbi Sandy Sasso, quoted in Sue Washburn, *Presbyterians Today*, June/July 2004, pp. 25–28.

Rationale for Conducting Tot Shabbat

Elyse Frishman

A synagogue community grows from three seeds: Torah (engaging with our tradition of wisdom), *g'milut chasadim* (living compassionately), and *avodah*. *Avodah*, "worship," enables spiritual development, reinforcing the preciousness of each person through the context of the congregation. We discover that we are neither invisible nor alone, that we are cared for even as we care for others. Through our liturgy, music, and Torah study, we gain perspective on our lives.

Shabbat worship saves us. It renews and refreshes, preparing us for challenges that lie ahead. Most days of the week are consumed by what we need and want; Shabbat marks what we already have. So many blessings nourish us!

Participating in worship as a family is successful family time. Few other activities reinforce sacred values for a family, offering each person a renewed commitment to "good behavior" going home. Communal Shabbat worship also draws the family into community. Through contact with other congregants, and through prayer and study, we realize our problems are not unique; we gain support from each other, even as our presence offers support to others.

When children are young, it's difficult to bring them to a mainstream Shabbat service. Even within a community highly tolerant of young sounds, parents can be distracted by their children. When worship means spending the entire time hushing a child, it discourages return.

Offering different worship opportunities draws in different constituencies. But it eliminates the single worshiping community. Especially in a smaller congregation, this may be divisive. Yet, the alternative is no communal Shabbat experience for parents whose youngest child may inhibit their participation.

Three near-simultaneous and significant changes taking place in the Reform community in the 1970s influenced the development of Tot Shabbat in the early 1980s* by increasing awareness of diversity in our ranks: the publication

---

*Young children had not been ignored by the Reform Jewish community, including the Women of Reform Judaism's Cradle Roll program and early childhood services in classical Reform

of *Gates of Prayer*, the ordination of women rabbis, and the ordination of a new generation of clergy, male and female, raised in the URJ (then UAHC) camping system and North American Federation of Temple Youth (NFTY). *Gates of Prayer* offered multiple services for multiple groups. Women rabbis drew attention to reframing how we welcomed our youngest children into worship. And for clergy influenced by camp and NFTY, there was an increased desire to develop worship suited to the spirituality of different age groups, partially in response to the phenomenon of campers returning from inspirational summer worship to "staid" synagogue worship. These same clergy in suburban settings were also urging their ritual committees to reconsider the time of Friday evening services; 7:30 P.M. was too early for commuters and too late for young families. Sanctuaries were filled with worship experiments, attempting to draw in those who had been disenfranchised spiritually.

Some congregations began experimenting with a worship setting for families with pre-readers. Young families would attend at a time more convenient for their children; taking into account a young child's attention span, the worship would be abbreviated; and the worship would be age-inclusive, engaging children and parents—Tot Shabbat. It stemmed from the realization that young children are spiritual and mindful. It was a learning opportunity, in the immediacy of the experience and in the long-term inculcation of prayer knowledge and Torah values.

Different models emerged: with or without a siddur, Torah, storytelling, arts and crafts, games, refreshment. Ultimately, a particular Tot Shabbat experience would be defined and shaped by the underlying principles of a particular community's worship vision. Changing the siddur from the *Union Prayer Book* to *Gates of Prayer* demonstrated a new attention to diversity, and original Tot Shabbat experiences mirrored this.

The different paradigm of *Mishkan T'filah's* two-page layout with alternative prayer choices teaches that diverse worshipers can pray together. So is Tot Shabbat still necessary? Yes, because the two primary and unique reasons for Tot Shabbat's necessity continue to be sensitivity to a young child's attention span and bedtime. But the crafting of Tot Shabbat will impact the expectations and transition of its worshipers to the mainstream worship environment. And it is a challenge for a family when one of multiple children outgrows Tot Shabbat. Will the family need to split up, a parent bringing a young child to Tot Shabbat while older children attend a different service?

Tot Shabbat should be spiritually transforming for *everyone* present. One telling sign of breakdown is when parents stop sitting with their children and begin to cluster away. Perhaps they say that "It's to allow our children to be with their friends"; more likely they are not engaged by the worship and have bowed out, giving their children over to us. Tot Shabbat must engage everyone. It must feel inclusive and attentive to those present while setting expectations that build community—a disciplined classroom per se.

The question of offering "Family Worship" should become moot. Offering a "Rock Shabbat" one week and "Family Shabbat" another will inform a

---

settings. The concept of worship aimed specifically at families with young children, with recognition of their particular needs, was new.

worshiper *when to stay away* as well as when to attend. The goal should be inclusivity. Expecting good parenting, and tolerance from seniors, will build a more sacred *k'hilah*. Everyone in the sanctuary can be engaged through carefully selected music and teaching. One avenue for understanding how to accomplish this is to consider the ability of the *sh'liach tzibur* to pray during Tot Shabbat. If worship offers the opportunity to connect with one another meaningfully, reinforcing values and community, reminding each person present, including the worship leader, that we are bound to each other and elevated as a whole by something greater than *our* whole—then yes, the *sh'liach tzibur* must pray, even during Tot Shabbat. If the liturgy or music is too banal and puerile for the leader, it is also beneath the parents and older children, who then are denied worship. Tot Shabbat also reminds the facilitator of the importance in connecting with each worshiper, a skill sometimes neglected when participants are expected to "get with the program." The same patience, guidance, and attentiveness extended to our young families will serve facilitators well in other worship settings.

Tot Shabbat helps to shape the Jewish identity of the young child, and the older sibling and parent. For the young child, it cultivates cultural affinity: vocabulary, music, prayers, values, ritual objects, and setting. Identifying Judaism as "mine" and being Jewish as "me" and "us" set the tone for life. Prayer opens a young child to talk with and about God and to appreciate this as normal dialogue. (There's plenty of time later on for an adolescent faith wrestling.) Young children deserve the sacred time and place to deepen their sense of God in their lives.

The experience of meaningful worship reinforces the Jewish value of being precious without being the center of the universe. Learning Torah, praying the *Sh'ma*, offering thanksgiving and even a healing prayer, a child learns that self-esteem can grow from what he or she can offer others. Older siblings and parents absorb this too. As children grow, numerous activities compete for their and their parents' attention. Tot Shabbat begins to inculcate a spirit of Shabbat at an early family age.

So here's what to avoid at Tot Shabbat:

- Pediatric Torah: Children's concerns often mirror our own. It's important to find common ground and articulate life's challenges and joys for young children and parents alike during Torah study. Telling the story of Noah's ark could include discussion about how parents protect their children. Learning about the Temple sacrifices could reference what we do to demonstrate our gratitude, discussing *tzedakah* and *g'milut chasadim*.
- Entertainment: "If Judaism is fun, they'll come back." Programming worship on a regular basis is exhausting and nearly impossible to sustain. The goal is to develop replicable worship that is learnable and engaging. Reinforce the values of family, caring community, living Torah, and counting blessings. Jewish prayer does this in its liturgy, and it is the liturgy that underpins Jewish worship. Develop meaningful worship without smoke and mirrors. Learn everyone's name. Translate *Modim* by inviting thanksgiving offerings from children and adults. Teach parents and grandparents how to bless their children; let them hug each other. (Have the grandparents bless and hug *their* children if multiple generations are present!)

- The inclination to create a new prayer book: Young children don't read. Parents do; use the siddur, or make a laminated prayer card with the Hebrew and transliteration. Avoid creative English prayers; they're unnecessary, and often the language is simply, well, childish. Focus instead on teaching the meaning of a prayer. Sing and chant, share prayers for the community, and study Torah. Teach children (and parents) sanctuary etiquette. Don't just give children stuffed Torah toys to parade; let them sit on the floor with the Torah unwrapped upon their laps and learn reverence through contact.

Determine what should be experienced during Tot Shabbat by considering what will be experienced in the other worship environment(s) these families will grow into, including Hebrew prayers and beloved congregational melodies; *kavod laTorah*, appropriate behavior; respect for one another and the larger community; attendance to the needs and concerns of all; the celebration of what is good and sacred. Tot Shabbat will help young families flow into the mainstream of congregational worship.

Like all Shabbat worship, Tot Shabbat should help us to set aside our needs and concerns and focus on our blessings: hands ready to help, hearts eager to love, lives to be cherished. Children and adults alike should leave Tot Shabbat feeling appreciated and loved, prepared to engage with all that might lie before them, growing spiritually into their years.

Part II

Who Are Our Youngest Congregants?

3

The Age of Awe and Wonder: Nurturing Meaning Making in Young Children

Roberta Louis Goodman

When our daughter Shoshana was a young child, in those days when she only spoke few words, my husband would take her to the shelf in our home where the Shabbat ritual objects were displayed. She would take the ritual objects off the shelf, and together they would bring them to the table. One Saturday night when my husband and I were going out and leaving her with the au pair, Shoshana took her father by the hand, led him to the Shabbat ritual objects, and motioned for him to lift her up so that she could take them off the shelf. She brought them to the dinner table and set them there. Admittedly, one other Saturday night when the scenario repeated itself, instead of going for the Shabbat ritual objects, she put her diaper bag on the table by the door that led to the garage. In both cases, in her preverbal way, she associated symbols and rituals with certain behaviors and ideas and used them to communicate an important message: "Don't leave me out!"

Young children have access to the raw material for fostering spiritual or faith development in a way that adults do not. In everything that they do, from learning to speak, to going to bed, they are gaining an understanding of their relationship to the world. The world is new and fresh. They are curious and open to new experiences. The smallest feat becomes a huge accomplishment. The challenge is: how do we as educators, parents, and teachers nurture their spiritual or faith development?

This chapter focuses on two sets of questions:

1. What can we learn from theorists about children's spiritual and faith development? What can we learn about adults, both parents and teachers, who nurture that development?
2. How can we approach fostering spiritual or faith development? What strategies should we consider?

In order to answer these questions, this chapter will present the following: (1) a presentation of Fowler's theory of faith development in regard to both young children and adults, (2) the implications of Vygotsky's sociohistorical theory of development, focusing on tools for nurturing faith development, and (3) some final thoughts on the role of progressive and constructivist education in nurturing meaning making.

Fowler's Faith Development Theory

A key developmental theorist in terms of spiritual or faith development is James W. Fowler. As a minister, Fowler was interested in the life stories of people and noticed patterns in how people framed their life experience. Fowler interviewed people of different ages, genders, and religious traditions in coming up with his stage theory of faith development that focuses on how people make meaning of their lives (Fowler, 1981). Fowler compiled his findings and presented his ideas about the developmental process in faith in his 1981 publication, *Stages of Faith.*

While his theory is called "faith development," Fowler notes that faith is really a process, an ongoing activity, and should be a verb, not a noun. "Faith or 'faithing' is the process by which a person finds and makes meaning of life's significant questions and issues, adheres to this meaning and acts it out in his or her life" (Goodman, 1985, p. 1). Faith development is one of few developmental theories that is both implicitly and explicitly compatible with religious language and ideas.

Key Ideas about Faith Development

- **All people are meaning makers.** We are meaning makers from birth, if not even while we are in the womb. Meaning making is the quality that defines us as human beings wherever or whenever (across time) we may live. Whether one is religious or an atheist, we all act as theologians or philosophers when we try to make sense of our existence. The stance that all individuals are meaning makers overcomes the split between rationality and passion, religion and secularism that has characterized modernity since the Enlightenment.
- **Making meaning grows and changes throughout our lifetime.** Just as we grow intellectually, socially, emotionally, and physically over time, so too do our faith, meaning making, and spirituality evolve. Both how we structure our faith and the content of our faith can develop and change throughout our lifetime.
- **Faith is about the whole person.** Unlike other theories that deal with only certain parts of human development, meaning making incorporates the intellectual, social, emotional, physical, and spiritual. Just as faith binds together these aspects, so, too, these aspects can be conduits through which faith is nurtured.
- **Faith is relational.** Even though faith is a personal quality, it is formed through our interactions with other individuals and groups. We are

influenced by our parents, teachers, coaches, friends, and peers, as well as our youth groups, teams, schools, congregations, and neighborhoods, and, unfortunately for some, by gangs and cults.

- **Faith formation involves shared centers of value and power.** These centers of value and power can be everything from the pursuit of fame, wealth, and beauty to the pursuit of *tikkun olam, g'milut chasadim* (loving-kindness), and holiness. The significance that we assign to these values is indicative of who we are and how we conduct our lives. These shared centers of value and power mediate the interactions between an individual and others, either individuals or groups. As people relate to one another, they are transmitting messages, either implicitly or explicitly, about what is important to them—what values and powers guide their lives.

- **Faith is both universal and particular.** Even though making meaning is a universal condition of human beings, people form their faith by choosing a particular path. This includes the possibility of being influenced by a religious and/or cultural tradition in pursuing this universal phenomenon. We do not go through faith stages in the abstract. Each individual's meaning making is filled with particular ideas, beliefs, experiences, practices, symbols, rituals, and customs.

- **Faith has a narrative quality.** We constantly create and revise stories about who we are and what is important in our lives. These stories encompass and reveal our meaning-making efforts, what are our values, commitments, struggles, and hopes. These stories give direction to our lives, informing our daily choices, long-term decisions, and actions.

Stage Theory

Faith changes throughout our lifetimes, both in its content and structure. Fowler presents his theory in terms of stages that identify key structural characteristics and changes. Since this theory focuses on how people structure their faith rather than the particular content of that faith, it can be applied to everyone.

Like other stage theories, the stages of faith are sequential and hierarchical. Sequential implies that people go through them in the same order. Hierarchical means that each stage builds on the previous one.

Fowler outlines one pre-stage and six "stages of faith." While age is not directly connected to stage, most people will reach at least stage 2 by the teenage years—with the onset of post-operational thinking and the ability to think abstractly—and few people will reach stage 6—universalizing faith, which is achieved primarily by martyrs and tzaddikim (righteous individuals), whose lives are dedicated entirely to others.

The pre-stage of meaning making begins at birth and continues until about eighteen months. Stage 1 is most typical of young children ages three to seven, the time when a child might be in an early childhood program. Stage 1 also includes the time when children will generally experience the onset of object permanence (ages six to eight), when they will begin to be able to distinguish reality from fantasy (e.g., the tooth fairy).

While young children will be in the pre-stage or perhaps stage 1, adults can be in stages 2, 3, 4, or even 5. In other words, children and adults are going to be at different stages in their development; they are not structuring faith in the same way. These differences present educational challenges in nurturing faith. By understanding how people construct faith, we can better address how to nurture faith.

The Six Stages of Faith

The choice, and perhaps the obligation, is for us as educators, parents, and teachers to take an active role in creating the space and conditions that will nurture children's meaning-making processes. The goal from Fowler's perspective is not to move them from one stage to another, but rather to fill it out, to make each stage a rich and deep experience. As Jewish educators, we want each child's meaning-making processes to be full of the experiences, stories, ideas, values, rituals, and symbols that include encounter and engagement with Judaism. Otherwise, we miss the opportunity to make Judaism an organic, foundational part of people's lives from "the beginning."

Through Jewish experiences like Tot Shabbat, as well as other early childhood Jewish programming, we can create a context and an environment that teach and model the worth and joy of living as a Jew while allowing children to construct their own connections to and understandings of Jewish life.

Fowler provides the framework for understanding what meaning making looks like at different stages in a child's life. While Fowler offers little insight in how to nurture these developmental stages, we can extrapolate practical educational applications from his theories. As mentioned above, there is one pre-stage and six main stages of faith. The pre-stage and first stage, which are most applicable to early childhood education, are summarized in the chart on the next page (based on Center for Faith Development, 1980; Fowler, 1981; Hayes, 1980; Goodman, 2002).

Implications for Nurturing Faith

Given the characteristics of faith stages and practical suggestions on how to nurture young children's meaning-making processes (especially their relationship to God and understanding of prayer), the following offers an educational approach to implementing Fowler's theory:

- **Start with examining your own meaning making.** A key step in nurturing young children's meaning making is for us as parents and/or Tot Shabbat leaders to explore our own meaning-making processes. It is essential not to underestimate how this exploration of ourselves—our own relationship to God and others, the role of prayer in our lives, our view of the world, and the values that guide our lives—affects nurturing our children's meaning making. The more that we reflect and raise questions about our lives, seek learning, and explore our own faith development, the more ready and open we are to hearing the questions about life that

Stage (Earliest Age Onset)	Characteristics	Implications for Nurturing Faith, Especially God and Prayer
Pre-stage: primal or undifferentiated faith (birth)	• Develop sense of trust through daily rituals. • Develop first images of the world as orderly or chaotic based on care provided. • Develop a sense of God based on trusting relationships with the caregiver.	• Introduce Jewish rituals, blessings, prayers; acknowledge moments of thanks and awe; include children in the performance of mitzvot (e.g., share special milestones or moments in children's lives with the *Shehecheyanu* prayer, other prayers, or songs). • As appropriate, allow children to experience these rituals through the five senses (e.g., kiss the Torah, smell the challah, march with the Torah). • Whether or not infants/toddlers actually "understand" what you are doing, they develop a sense of rhythm and how to relate to their world through your actions, reactions, and emotions. • In daily rituals, like eating and sleeping, introduce Jewish elements from the Tot Shabbat service (e.g., saying blessings, singing songs). • Use Jewish sources from the Tot Shabbat service throughout the day (e.g., play calming Jewish music at naptime, read Jewish books during storytime, point at people, places, and things in Hebrew and English).
Stage 1	• Use language to build relationships and control environment. • Differentiate self from others. • Rely on imagination and images to understand world. • Imitate rituals and roles. • Lured by symbols, the mysterious, or magical. • Respond with emotions and whole body, especially in prayer. • Obey out of a fear of punishment.	• Continue introducing rituals as with the prior stage, but allow children ample opportunity to practice rituals. They will imitate your actions. Use Hebrew pronunciations of ritual objects, prayers, and holidays as much as possible. In performing rituals, remember to take time to experience them through the senses, consider their mystery. • Emphasize concepts related to prayer, like gratitude, wonder, sanctifying time, or asking for health as they appear in the service or spontaneously (e.g., include the *Mi Shebeirach*—prayer for healing—for the types of "pains or ills" that affect children or their parents, including a sick pet, someone who has the flu, feeling sad when a visitor leaves; start the morning with *Modeh/Modah Ani*—thanking God for being alive each day—and emphasize that this can be done at home; introduce "prayer and tell" as part of the service where children can share something special for which the group says a blessing). • Ask families to bring in, talk about, and then use as part of the service one of their ritual objects (e.g., *Kiddush* cup, *yad*, challah cover from home, as it models and creates connections). • Use music and movement not just to sing prayers or songs about concepts related to blessings and prayers, but also to experience and explore with one's whole body feelings, meanings associated with different prayers. • Introduce the Jewish rhythm of time and connect it to the children's lives whenever possible (e.g., identify the Shabbat by the name of the weekly Torah portion, announce Rosh Chodesh with a prayer, celebrate the birthdays of children that fall during a Hebrew month). • Share different names for God. Explore what they mean (e.g., God as "Rock," Redeemer, Ruler). • Read Jewish stories—Bible, midrash, traditional and modern literature—about God. Have children express their feelings, ideas, and questions about these stories. Connect the ways that these figures relate to one another to the ways that we relate to others and vice versa.

our children are asking, what our children feel and think about God and prayer, and how our children are making sense of their place in the world. The more comfortable that you are with addressing your own questions and seeking, the more comfortable you will be in nurturing the faith of others; children will readily sense your comfort or discomfort.

• **Tap into "teachable" moments.** All of life is a stage for meaning making. Tapping into the natural flow of experiences by raising awareness through noticing, questioning, examining, and sanctifying are all part of helping children realize what is important in life and what are the sacred gifts of this world. It is important to take the time to acknowledge changes and accomplishments in children's lives, their moments of real connection with others, and their experiences with nature. These are all *"Shehecheyanu* moments" for connecting the everyday to the sacred.

• **Realize that listening, asking questions, and guiding are more important than answering.** We are constructors of the meaning of life, interpreters of our own experiences. We develop a sense of purpose from a very young age. When it comes to the "big questions," there is a tendency for adults to want to give the "right answer," when in fact, not only are there no "right" answers, but children are actually better served by our promoting the "quest" in questions and allowing them to come to their own conclusions. When children share their ideas, it is always important to be open to their answers—really hearing them, encouraging their exploration, and responding in a way that keeps them communicating and searching.

• **Use stories to stimulate meaning making.** We create stories about who we are and what is important in our lives. Judaism, like all traditions, cultures, religions, families, and institutions, has stories about what is important. The challenge is to help children make connections to these stories so that the "big story" becomes part of "my story" and, in doing so, these stories become dynamic for our time and place. Storytelling is an effective educational tool that allows children to construct their own meaning. Stories are not only a source of entertainment for children, they also provide a framework for understanding our world, raise important questions about morality and values, and offer different types of solutions to different types of situations. They are tools for provoking and, in the best sense of constructivist education, a place where the self can encounter Judaism and the world.

A Final Thought on Tot Shabbat and Adults

Educators who are planning for Tot Shabbat should also consider the developmental needs of the adult participants and the educational opportunities Tot Shabbat offers for them, as well as their children. The different stages of faith development in which different parents will fall will likely influence their reactions to Tot Shabbat. Some adults will find it a meaningful worship experience for themselves. Others may value it only for their children.

Tot Shabbat can fulfill different adult needs. It can serve as any of the following:

- An entry point or gateway for some adults to seeking other meaningful Jewish worship experiences or learning about Jewish prayer and praying.
- A place to learn about the service, making prayers and praying more accessible in a nonjudgmental, nonthreatening environment.
- A way to help parents think about and learn how they can nurture their children's spirituality, encounters with God, and meaning making at home.
- A way to create or enrich rituals in their homes.
- A step to helping parents experience leading parts of services, to being the leaders of Jewish ceremonies and celebrations in their homes as well as in the congregation.

Vygotsky's Theory of Social Historical Cognitive Development and Nurturing Faith

Today in North America, Lev Vygotsky is a popular theorist among educators of young children. In his work, he made important connections between development, learning, and schooling. His theories have come to light relatively recently, given that he was born in tsarist Russia and died in 1934 at the age of thirty-seven. Vygotsky was a Jew who confronted discrimination in his quest to attend university. He embraced the Marxist ideology that brought on the Russian Revolution and integrated it into his work. He viewed his theory of social historical cognitive development as a vehicle for building a new socialist society. Unfortunately for him, the Soviet officials did not share his optimism. Many of his writings were suppressed by the Soviet government until the mid-1960s. Only relatively recently have his writings become widely available in English.

Vygotsky said that human beings learn by inventing and using tools. Vygotsky's emphasis on the tools of one's social and historical context as a significant factor in fostering learning offers a way of thinking about how to nurture meaning making. Applying Vygotsky's theory to the task of nurturing meaning making asks us as Jewish educators to identify the tools of our time that can help bridge the gap between what children know and experience about Jewish life and what they can come to know and experience.

The Tools of Jewish Life

Judaism is rich in tools. Many tools exist that can help us nurture young children's meaning-making processes to experience the richness of Jewish life—culturally, religiously, morally, and spiritually. Some of these tools are geared more toward children, and others are tools for parents and Tot Shabbat leaders to use in preparing for the services and nurturing meaning making during the experience.

The following are some examples of Jewish tools:

- **Ritual objects** (e.g., mezuzah, *Kiddush* cup, *Havdalah* set, Torah scroll, tallit, menorah, sukkah): Ritual objects are connected both to ritual acts and to stories of the Jewish people. For example, the Torah service is a reenactment of the Jewish people receiving the Torah on Mount Sinai. Sharing these types of stories helps children make strong connections to the ritual objects and prayers of the Tot Shabbat service.

- **Hebrew or Jewish calendar:** The whole idea of Shabbat presents some key concepts about Jewish time, including some related to the Hebrew or Jewish calendar. Calendars are concrete items that help the leader think about the space used for Tot Shabbat. A calendar is just one of the tools that can be part of the physical setup. It has meaning-making implications with connections to the weekly Torah portion, announcing Rosh Chodesh (the new month), and identifying the beginning (sundown) and end of holidays (sunset).

- **Blessings and prayers:** Blessings and prayers are a way of assigning words and meaning to actions. They are another tool for connecting to key ideas about life, like giving thanks for everyday things (e.g., food, our bodies) and acknowledging wonder in our world (e.g., seeing a rainbow or smelling a blossom for the first time each year).

- **Names of God:** God may be "invisible" in the corporal sense, but the Torah and prayer book include many names for God that help us better understand what God is like. Children often relate to God as a Parent, but among the more than one hundred names for God are Ruler, Rock, and Creator. All these different ways to refer to God help us find different ways to relate to God.

- **Hebrew:** Language transmits culture and expresses how we look at the world. Hebrew is the language of prayer and the Bible. Using the Hebrew names of key values, like *tzedakah* (righteous act) or *g'milut chasadim* (deeds of loving-kindness), helps identify these as Jewish values.

- **Jewish books:** As Jews, we are considered the "People of the Book." Both traditional and contemporary Jewish books should be available to children. Children learn how to open a book in English and read from left to right, and they can just as easily learn the flow of reading Hebrew from right to left, see the shapes of Hebrew letters, and learn about the layout of a traditional text through picking up Jewish books. Compiling a list of books or stories shared at Tot Shabbat can help parents extend this experience into the home.

Why Are Tools So Important?

Tools are an important part of early childhood education for several reasons:

- **Using tools is a concrete and developmentally appropriate teaching technique.** Young children are concrete learners. Tools are concrete. Children experiment with and master "things" in the world around them. What surrounds them at a young age becomes part of the child's "natural" or "expected" world order. We see Jewish adults struggle with even knowing the names, shapes, and basic orientation of what some of these tools are, much less how to use them. The introduction of these tools could easily start at a young age.

- **Tools connect us to key concepts and messages of Jewish life and living.** While tools are concrete, they point to abstract ideas and concepts about Judaism and Jewish living. For example, the calendar is a tool for keeping track of time that conveys a sense of how Jews think about time. The seventh day on the Jewish calendar is Shabbat, a day to be sanctified, the day on which God rested from creation. Jews sanctify time—daily, weekly, monthly, yearly, and over one's lifetime—as reflected in our celebrations. As specific as each tool is, it points to something bigger or larger about life.

- **Tools open up future learning and growth.** Tools are a means to an end, in this case knowledge and hopefully commitment to a Jewish way of life. The ability to use tools makes us feel capable and competent as well as providing us with a basis to further our learning and growth.

- **Tools are a vehicle for experimenting, exploring, and interpreting Judaism.** Children should have the opportunity to explore the tools, their properties, uses, and histories or stories through the five senses in both conventional and unconventional ways. What spices would you put in a *Havdalah* spice box? How does an artist make a silver *Kiddush* cup? In what ways do people decorate Jewish calendars as compared to "general" calendars? What is something that has happened in your life that is special, and what blessing would you say for that experience? What makes God like a rock?

    As important as repetition and imitation are for acquiring tools, children need exposure to the "why" of the tools and not just the "what." Why do we light Shabbat candles, as well as how? Why do we say a blessing before we eat our food, as well as which is the correct blessing for which type of food? Why do we have a *yad* to read the Torah, as well as what is it made of? Investigating these "why" questions will help promote discovery and meaning making.

What Happens to Children Who Don't Have These Tools?

Through introducing the concept of "oppression of the masses," Karl Marx argued that the ownership of land and the tools to work that land were critical to reach one's full potential and fully participate in society, both economically and politically. In today's world, knowledge and the tools that aid knowing are the commodities that are necessary to thrive. This is also true in our Jewish lives. As individuals and as educators, we are faced with the challenge of asking and answering life's big questions. Having the ability to access and use the tools that Judaism provides, its sources and resources, is absolutely essential. It liberates us and makes us owners of and conversant with the most important commodity of our day—knowledge—and the tools that come with accessing that knowledge. Otherwise we risk being "oppressed" in the sense of being disenfranchised or incapable of navigating our own religious and cultural heritage or tradition as Jews as we seek meaning and purpose in our lives.

From a faith-development perspective, children whose pre-stage and stage 1 are not filled out in an environment rich in these Jewish resources and sources, whether that be at home, synagogue, school, or all of these combined, will miss out on making these tools part of how they create meaning from the beginning.

Clearly the young child will not learn or master all that is possible with any of these tools. Yet, while individuals can gain exposure, familiarity, and basic competency with these tools at another time in their life, an opportunity will have been missed. How much better it is to lay the foundation, memories, motivation, and comfort at a time when these resources and sources, the tools, are associated with awe and wonder and the "natural" order of one's world than at other times during the life span.

How Can Tot Shabbat Leaders Most Effectively Use and Share These Tools?

- **Parents and Tot Shabbat leaders need to be comfortable with using the tools, both traditional and contemporary, for their own meaning making.** Some may need to learn what some of these tools are. The ability of parents and Tot Shabbat leaders to tap into technological tools can make a huge difference in the accessibility of Jewish tools to children. Many adults struggle with using computers as much as they struggle with using ritual objects to create Jewish experiences. If adults are to help children use these tools to find meaning in their lives, then they too need to have opportunities to explore how these sources and resources can help them answer their own life questions.
- **Parents and Tot Shabbat leaders will need to learn about how children structure faith.** As indicated before, the way that an adult structures faith is different from how a young child structures faith. For the young child, awe and wonder are a dominant way of relating to the world. Parents and Tot Shabbat leaders tend to be much more rational, realistic, and linear in terms of their own faith development. They will need to understand how children create meaning.
- **Parents and Tot Shabbat leaders need to know how to use the tools not just to inform but to explore, to stimulate the natural curiosity that children have about their world.** As important as it is for children to master some of these tools, just teaching them by rote is not going to tap into the sense of wonder and awe that motivates and stimulates young children. Think of the difference between children counting to ten repeatedly, without a meaningful context, as compared to children counting to ten while trying to figure out how many of their classmates are absent from school or how many acorns they found in their backyard.

Adults can make it possible for children to reach their full potential by pursuing ongoing parent and professional development opportunities to expand their own knowledge and comfort with the tools of Jewish life, making a commitment to pursuing meaning making in their own lives, and increasing their understanding of faith development theory, including how to nurture faith.

What Tools Should Be Available in Tot Shabbat Settings?

Serious consideration needs to be given to the physical setup of the place where Tot Shabbat is held, especially in terms of the tools that are available to the children to explore. How can tools be used to help children make the transition from the "outside world" to the world of prayer and Shabbat and vice versa? What tools are we already giving to the families? What type of prayer book is distributed? Is Torah read? Which songs are sung? How much time do we give to the children to explore these tools? Do we give them real or artificial versions of these tools? Often ritual objects made of plastic or childproof materials are unaesthetic and look pretend as opposed to what one would hopefully find in a child's home. This too sends a message about what we think children are capable of handling and competent to interact with.

More critical, how are these ritual objects presented? Are they set out on a table as part of a display, or are they set up to promote curiosity, questioning, and investigation? Are they used only during the service for a limited few, or are they presented in a way that promotes discovery and addresses the why of their use and not just the how?

The potential for any of these tools to capture the imaginations of young children and incorporate them into their meaning-making processes is great. The question and challenge are whether we are fostering a sense of the sacred, religious and/or cultural imagination, and joy.

A Concluding Thought about the Role of Progressive and Constructivist Education in Nurturing Meaning Making

The educational key to nurturing meaning making, including effectively using traditional and contemporary tools, can be found in progressive and constructivist educational approaches. Progressive education emphasizes many principles that are compatible with the individual construction of meaning. Some of these principles include learning by doing, using real-life material and experiences, and encouraging experimentation and independent thinking (Mooney, 2000, p. 4).

An increasingly popular approach to early childhood education, within the Jewish community and throughout the world, comes from the educators of Reggio Emilia, a town in Italy. This constructivist approach is characterized by ideas such as the following:

- Children are capable and competent.
- Learning should be child centered and not teacher centered.
- Children express themselves through "100 languages."
- The teacher is a researcher, observing and reflecting back the words and images of children's learning.
- The environment is a "third teacher."
- The whole community is both responsible for and part of the learning experience

This approach has its roots in the progressive movement of John Dewey and others. It is an approach that sees children as interpreters of their own experiences and schools as an opportunity to deepen and enrich that exploration. May all of our young children and their families have the opportunity to experience this type of learning, which can create a dynamic experience of Jewish life in their quest for meaning.

Bibliography

Center for Faith Development. Chart of Fowler's Stages of Faith with stage name, representative picture of the stage, and dominant faith development issues. Handout, Emory University, 1980.

Crain, William. *Theories of Development: Concepts and Applications*. 4th edition. Upper Saddle River, NJ: Prentice Hall, 2000.

Fowler, James W. *Stages of Faith: The Psychology of Human Development and the Quest for Meaning*. San Francisco: Harper & Row Publishers, 1981.

Goodman, Roberta Louis. "Developmental Psychology." In *The Ultimate Jewish Teachers Handbook*, edited by Nachama Moskowitz, pp. 85–108. Springfield, NJ: A.R.E. Publishing, 2003.

Goodman, Roberta Louis. "Nurturing a Relationship to God and Spiritual Growth: A Developmental Approach." In *Teaching about God and Spirituality*, edited by Roberta Louis Goodman and Sherry Blumberg. Denver: A.R.E. Publishing, 2002.

Hayes, Nancy. Unpublished chart of Fowler's Stages of Faith listing stage name, Erikson's Life Cycle phase, ages, and characteristics. Tulsa, OK, 1980.

Mooney, Carol Garhart. *An Introduction to Dewey, Montessori, Erikson, Piaget & Vygotsky*. St. Paul, MN: Redleaf Press, 2000.

4

Building a Jewish Brain, Nurturing a Jewish Heart

Ellen Allard and Peter Allard

The human brain begins to develop shortly after conception. By the time a baby takes that first breath, the lower regions of the brain, the spinal cord and the brain stem, are very well developed. However, at birth, even though the brain has undergone a remarkable amount of development, there is still much growth to take place. The higher regions—the limbic system and the cerebral cortex— have some catching up to do.

Most certainly, you have a legitimate right to ask what brain development has to do with Tot Shabbat. The answer is: **Everything!** But our aim is not to convince you that Tot Shabbat can make your young worshipers have a higher IQ. Our goal is to help you understand that Tot Shabbat is one piece of a beautiful, multicolored quilt of experiences that will contribute to a child's overall development.

The thing about babies and young children in general is that every new impulse, sensation, and feeling experienced is registered and stored in the gray stuff between their ears. Each new stimulus matters, whether they are conscious of the information being processed or not. Light, wind, sound, cloth, skin, being held and fed and changed and clothed and burped and every single thing, particularly when it happens for the first time in a child's life—all of it is new. And then, because of repetition, perspective is gained. This occurs when the information or stimuli are assessed. The moment-to-moment, day-to-day routines and practices that children experience and learn on their long journey to self-sufficiency are stored, allowing the brain to do the incredible work of processing, judging, assessing, and distinguishing one event from another, rank ordering them as to fun, exciting, dangerous, hot, cold, sleepy, scary, and so on. These connections and judgments made during the very earliest times in our lives contribute strongly to the adult that each of us is today.

Think of the brain in terms of an Internet search engine. To date, there are approximately 700 billion pages available on the Web. Despite this almost unfathomable number of pages, we can find virtually anything in mere moments, instantly creating connections that provide us with information unknown only a few moments before. A young child's every living moment can be compared to the World Wide Web—it is made up of billions of pages that are sorted and catalogued within their brain, even though the filters that create these connections and opinions are either not yet formed or slowly evolving. It is vital that those who care for young children, whether it be parents, caregivers, teachers, or worship leaders, be ever aware that these connections are being made during every single moment of a child's life.

Brain Development Crash Course

Babies are born with billions of brain cells called neurons. You would think that the large number of neurons present at birth would make for a very large brain! In reality, the brain is only about one-quarter of its full size at birth. By the time a child is three years old, the brain is about 80 percent full grown, and by age five, 90 percent, continuing to grow until about age thirty. Lest you think it ends there, brain cells can continue developing throughout life. Keep doing those crossword and sudoku puzzles!

Neurons are critical for brain development. When neurons communicate with each other, synapses are created. Synapses help neurons stay alive. Neurons that aren't involved in synaptic activity are pruned away. This process has been referred to as the "use it or lose it" principle or what neuroscientists call the "cells that fire together, wire together" rule. While this sounds harsh, there is a certain amount of normal pruning of brain cells; this allows those that remain to be more efficient and is in fact a part of brain development that continues throughout life, though it's far more common in early childhood. In less optimal situations, when children are deprived of normal, healthy experiences in their early years, an overpruning of connections can take place, seriously altering brain development.

How does the whole neuron thing work? Neurons sprout dendrites. Dendrites are the receivers for synapses from other neurons. Axons are the pathways upon which synapses travel between neurons. Myelin is the material that coats the axons and enables them to be productive. Think of a neighborhood full of houses, with telephone wires strung on poles throughout the streets (or underneath the ground). The houses are the neurons, the doors are the dendrites, and the telephone wires are the axons. Let's say that neighbor number one decides to visit neighbor number two. She picks up the phone and calls her neighbor, her neighbor answers the phone, and they plan a visit. Neighbor number two arrives at neighbor number one's door, rings the bell, and is invited in for tea. Voilà! A synapse was created. But if the wires aren't in good shape, the neighbors won't be able to speak by phone with each other because of the crackling and static on the line, and a visit won't be planned. In order for the phone call to take place, the wires need to be in good shape—just like the myelination of the axons, which, if conditions are optimal, will set the stage for healthy brain development. So, make sure your telephone company keeps your telephone wires in good shape!

In order to maximize brain development and keep those neurons firing, children need adequate nutrition; loving, stable, and responsive adults; and a rainbow of developmentally and age-appropriate experiences. In a child's first five years, an astounding array of abilities, skills, and insights will emerge. The groundwork for this growth can be augmented by your consistent and carefully designed Tot Shabbat services. By providing this for the young children in your congregation, you will set the stage for healthy synaptic connections to be made, thus fostering and nurturing the neural connections that will enable cognitive, linguistic, social-emotional, physical, and spiritual development to take place.

Before that can happen, it must be stressed that a very important aspect of brain development is related to safety. Initially, a young child's (it doesn't stop when infants become toddlers) most primal and basic interest lies in feeling safe. Because physical safety gets top billing, the brain categorizes early events based on predictability and reliability. Once a child can rely on his needs being met in a loving and consistent manner, he can turn his attention to exploring the world and all the surrounding stimuli. The brain is then free to make more and new connections between events.

Music and Biology

When we lead Tot Shabbat services, we see the power that music has on every person present—children and adults alike. Music can influence mood, bring listeners and participants to laughter or tears, and cause all those within hearing distance to move, even if they aren't aware of their movements. Surely, you've found yourself toe tapping to a song even before you realized you were doing it.

From a physiological standpoint, music evokes emotion, which is followed by a buildup of neurochemicals in the brain. When the music is accompanied by movement, whether deliberate or not, it releases the neurochemicals, providing an outlet that enables us to maintain our equilibrium. Movement can evoke emotion as well and by its very nature has a built-in mechanism for releasing built-up neurochemicals in the brain. Thus, a combination of music and movement can elicit emotional connections that have the potential to find a permanent and long-lasting place in a child's heart and brain.

Singing, which is what we are referring to when we speak about music as it relates to Tot Shabbat, can alter brain chemistry and is directly associated with well-being, stress reduction, and immune system strength. When people sing together, they experience a significant increase in a neurochemical in the brain called oxytocin, found to increase bonds of trust between people, clearly explaining why singing in a group can be so powerful and intimately moving. But wait, there is more that the brain can do: the brain has an automatic tendency to also find a cause for the exhilarating feelings brought on by oxytocin. Our brains insist on finding a reason for a change in our stasis. If a child participating in a group activity sees smiling faces, dancing bodies, and joyous singing, the child's brain doesn't attribute the good feelings to oxytocin. The credit goes to the singing and dancing and gathering of people who are sharing the good feelings! That is why people created societies in the first place. With a successful music- and movement-filled Tot Shabbat, oxytocin could be the motivation for people joining your synagogue. Music and physiology—a powerful combination!

Safe and Loving Prayerful Experiences

Let's consider what is most needed for optimal brain development as it relates to Tot Shabbat: loving experiences full of language and music and beautiful colors in an environment that invites exploration and is a constant source of safety and reliability. Quite simply—hold and hug and dance with children, sing and laugh and talk to children, respond to children's needs quickly and lovingly. And this doesn't end when babies become toddlers or when toddlers become preschoolers. These rich and constant experiences are vitally important for optimal brain development throughout a young child's life. In fact, it follows that many of the choices we make from our youngest years stem directly from deeply held perceptions formed as young children. Years of therapy will not undo some of those beliefs!

Knowing about the need for very young children to feel safe, those who plan Tot Shabbat services for young children and their families can begin by addressing this need and examining every possible factor that goes into these events. Certainly, the content of your service must be age appropriate. But remember that there are many other important details that factor into creating a pleasurable, safe, predictable, and repeatable experience for each child: lighting, room temperature, colors, seating, the sound system, aromatherapy (mmmhhh, can you smell the freshly baked challah?), not to mention the greetings and attitudes of the adults who welcome the children and their parents to the space. For each child, all stimuli are catalogued, sorted, connected, and processed, quickly becoming judgments that reflect safe or unsafe, good or bad, like or dislike.

Once this has been established and assured, then the power of music can do the work it does so beautifully, hardwiring those feelings and experiences deep within the brain. It can increase alertness through blasts of norepinephrine and epinephrine, serotonin and dopamine and endorphins. This cocktail makes us feel good, energized, communal, and loving. And the end result is an experience that has the power to create long-lasting memories and connections for all of your youngest worshipers.

There is no wasted time in a child's life. The adults who plan and/or lead Tot Shabbat services must take full advantage of the opportunity and time to consciously, considerately, and clearly establish programs and public worship events that will support the goals we all have: to share the wonder and joy of our faith, of our people, and of our work.

5

Do You Speak Three-Year-Old?

Nancy Bossov

I once had a conversation with a rabbi following a Tot Shabbat service the rabbi led at the synagogue's early childhood center. We chatted about the session, and I tried to provide constructive suggestions about how to improve on providing the children with a meaningful, lively, and memorable Tot Shabbat experience. We talked about some very important issues, particularly how to prepare for Tot Shabbat. The key reason why this rabbi did not have a successful Tot Shabbat service was because she had come to Tot Shabbat for forty children without a plan, without a list of songs, without a story to tell, without questions to ask, without a roster of the children's names, without pictures from her recent vacation to share, without pictures of her baby to show, without a discussion in advance with any of the teachers about what the children had been working on in class all week. There had been no thought about any potential connecting points between the rabbi and the children. These children are congregants too. Teaching them requires just as much preparation as teaching adults or leading a regular Shabbat service—some would say it takes even more preparation, especially if one does not have a lot of experience or comfort working with very young children.

When any instructor prepares, he or she considers the whole situation: the setup of the room, the time of day, the circumstances under which the participants are there, the amount of time they will have together, the information communicated in advance of the "event," the expectations of all parties, the goals of the time together, the acoustics, the anticipated hunger of the crowd, the attention span, the instructor's familiarity with the place, people, rituals, music, and history of previous experiences with the group, the range of knowledge among the group, the mood and spirit of the community, country, and world. When preparing Tot Shabbat, it is also extremely important to have a working knowledge of what is developmentally appropriate for young children. How do young children learn? How do they participate best? What are they able to learn and understand? Young children grow and change very quickly, but we need to know what is age appropriate for them in order to create a successful Tot Shabbat experience.

A Developmental Scan from the Perspective of the Children Themselves

Eighteen to Twenty-four Months Old

Children of this age are very excited to go anywhere with their families. Going to a new place like the synagogue or the sanctuary is exciting and stimulating but may also be a little scary. If Tot Shabbat is at the end of the day, these children might be on their second wind after a nap, but by the end of the evening, they may be pretty tired and grumpy. If Tot Shabbat is in the morning, they will have a lot of energy and be bursting with enthusiasm. Some children this age who are a bit more shy might find the whole Tot Shabbat experience a bit overwhelming at first. It may take shyer children a couple of services before they start to feel comfortable. When children this age enter a large room with a big open space, even if that space is between the pews and the ceiling, they will have the urge to run. When they see other children, they become even more excited, and the urge to run around is even stronger. It takes someone with very catchy tunes or stories to grab and keep their attention. Once they are allowed to start running around the room and getting all wound up, it is very hard for them to settle back down. Finding the "Shabbat feeling" is pretty much over after that.

Most children of this age are not yet able to express their feelings and needs verbally. They are more prone to frustration because of their inability to get across what they are feeling to the grown-ups around them. They use their bodies to learn, explore, and express their feelings. It's really helpful to sing songs about thoughts and feelings that include movement because that helps them communicate in a way that they can. As the children grow older and more verbal, this is a bridge between communicating with bodies and facial expressions and the use of language. The use of simple songs, rhymes, and stories—especially where a child fills in a word or action at just the right time to complete the idea—makes the children feel really important and successful. Children this age love to be given important "jobs" during the service. Whatever these jobs are (e.g., holding a puppet or a toy Torah, passing out song sheets), they teach children the Jewish value of helping others, being part of a community, and all the ways we can serve God.

Two to Three Years Old

Two- to three-year-olds are becoming much more verbal. They can communicate more and more each day and love to use their new verbal skills. Unfortunately, they feel no social constraints about what is "appropriate" or not. They are truly honest in all that they say and do, and their feelings are very sensitive. They are becoming more and more curious about everything around them. Curiosity drives their need to explore the world around them through play. They like to be in command of their environment and manipulate objects to be just where they want them. That includes other children. When they arrive at Tot Shabbat, they expect to be at the center of the service and will do everything they can during the service to let everybody know that they are supposed to be paying attention to them, and not the rabbi or cantor or song leader or teacher. If they have a special role or job during the service, their developmental needs might be met and they won't feel as strong a need for attention. They might also be more interested in the leader who gave them the special job and the attention that went with it. Some examples of jobs include carrying the *sifrei Torah* (stuffed dolls) during a *hakafah*, holding puppets or other props during the story, holding up a pointer finger for number one for the *Sh'ma*, or helping a parent light Shabbat candles.

The two- to three-year-olds' increasing physical agility, enthusiasm, and natural ego drive to participate can make a leader's job challenging or can make them wonderful Tot Shabbat participants. Now that these children are developing verbally, they can participate more fully in social situations. This means that they want to participate in activities where they can speak, sing, and repeat after anybody who asks them to. They love silly word games too. They feel accomplished when they are able to use their new verbal skills. But be aware, they are not so skilled at holding back. If they have an idea or something to say and they can say it, you can be sure they will, no matter what is going on at the time. They are not concerned about interrupting others or even answering the particular question you asked.

Some two- to three-year-olds are more hesitant to use all these new verbal and physical skills. Some feel secure staying close to parents and observing all the action. These children can participate from afar and often learn more than we realize from watching. They can feel part of the experience and connected with the leaders and the group even though they are not participating in all the action. It is important for a leader to respect each child's choices and style. Children will choose to let go of Mom or Dad and participate more fully in singing and physical activities when they are ready. It is important to remember that every child is on his or her own developmental timetable.

Three Years Old

Now that these children have been walking and talking and running and jumping for almost two years, they are experts. They do not consider themselves babies anymore. They feel quite capable and quite curious. They are deep thinkers and love to ask a lot of questions. Their favorite question is "why?" This is not a question to be taken lightly; they want an answer with as much depth as you can give them in concrete language. This is very challenging and can make adults uncomfortable. Three-year-olds want serious answers but framed in an age-appropriate way. When they ask difficult questions, adults will often smile and seem really surprised, but then find some kind of excuse to change the subject. The children quickly realize that adults are uncomfortable with their questions. Children of this age are natural theologians. They have a very intuitive sense of God, feel comfortable talking about God, and want to know more about God. It is better to tell three-year-olds that you don't know the answer to their questions than to avoid the question or change the subject. It's also perfectly reasonable to let them know that people and great scholars have been asking the very same questions for hundreds or thousands of years. They would probably like to know this. It puts them in a very select group of thinkers!

Don't hesitate to ask them what they think. You will often be amazed by their ideas and opinions. What is most important is to be open to questions and discussion and try to use concrete language if possible (avoid metaphors and vocabulary words they will not understand). The fun is in the wonder of it all, not the answers (since there really aren't any!).

Children of this age are learning to take turns and improve their listening skills. These two activities are very challenging. They watch and imitate others, so having good models helps a lot. They love integrating play with pretend and constructing, deconstructing, collaborating with others on a project, story, or song, and building one idea into another idea. These skills grow as the year goes on and they mature. They really like to role-play different characters and try on different roles with their friends. If they enjoy Tot Shabbat, they might try being the rabbi or song leader conducting a Tot Shabbat in dramatic play in school.

Four Years Old

Four-year-olds are "the big kids on campus." They are the big kids at school and are preparing to go to kindergarten! Although they have huge emotional moments of insecurity, especially with their friends, they have honed their social skills. They feel pretty accomplished and confident in their verbal, physical, emotional, and cognitive skills. They are still very curious and love to ask questions, and if they are in a nurturing, supportive, and encouraging environment, they will try to figure out the answers to their own questions.

Four-year-olds have learned a lot about group organizational and social rules, so you can expect them to be able to sit in a group and take turns listening. They will wait for their turn to contribute to the goings-on, and if you forget to call on them, they will remind you! They are still curious about God and have their own ideas about what, who, how, and even why we have a God and why God has us. Adults who talk with them seriously about God may be amazed. Children of this age have often internalized their own philosophy of God by listening, observing, questioning, and modeling those same adults!

Four-year-olds think a lot about their future and like to "try on" different roles. They need their friends to work with them on this, so they will take turns playing out each other's ideas: "I'll play post office with you if you'll play school with me"; "No, I want to be the teacher; you be the student"; "OK, you are the zookeeper, and we'll all pretend to be different animals at the zoo." Their imaginations take them to all kinds of places. This is why children this age love stories. Don't be surprised if they enjoy your story so much that they get a little ahead of where you thought you were going!

Five Years Old

Five-year-olds may not be sure that they belong at Tot Shabbat anymore, and yet they still enjoy it and get a lot out of being there. They may feel that they don't belong there with the "babies," but they can be encouraged to take on new roles. They will also enjoy being able to answer so many questions. They still love being with their families, and trips to temple together are meaningful for them.

Five-year-olds continue to build on important skills like sharing, expressing feelings and needs, and understanding social rules. They have a good understanding of when they should be quiet and listen and when it's OK to talk and give their opinion. They love to have a job and feel really important. When they do something and everybody tells them they did a good job, they feel so good and important, like a real grown-up. They are independent in so many ways. Their friends are very important to them.

Suggestions for Tot Shabbat Planning and Speaking Three-Year-Old

Leading Tot Shabbat is incredibly rewarding, but it is also demanding. Connecting with young children requires a lot of energy, serious preparation, but also a willingness to "go with the flow." Take the time to prepare, but then be sure to enjoy!

This may sound easier said than done but before stepping into a Tot Shabbat, stop, take a breath, and remember: this is your *Gan Eden*, your oasis of civilization for twenty to thirty minutes. It is your opportunity to behave, engage, interact, model, and touch the hearts of the Tot Shabbat congregation. You will connect with the children as you move your body, because your eyes meet theirs, because your warm touch soothes them, because your enthusiasm transmits the connections between heart, mind, and soul, and because your voice represents the words of Torah from the past into the present and future.

This chapter has given you some guidelines for how young children develop, but it's important to remember that every child is different. Accept each one of the Tot Shabbat participants for who they are, where they are, how they are, and why they are there. Remember that there are no wrong answers—even when a child gives an "answer" that has nothing to do with your question. If every child feels valued (and not judged), they will continue to be open to asking and answering your questions and will partipate wholeheartedly.

Never use sarcasm. Young children do not understand it, but they do hear the tone of it and it will hurt their feelings. Good humor is essential unless it is at the expense of some individual or group. It is important to be clear to whom you are speaking. It is OK at points to share information with the adults that you know the children won't understand. They should be there to learn as well. Speaking three-year-old does not mean using "baby talk" or "dumbing it down." Try to avoid using metaphors, as they are confusing. Be as concrete as possible. Clear language without difficult vocabulary or idioms will work best. Don't worry if you occasionally use a word that a child doesn't know—he or she will ask you what it means. Your full sentences and clear logical communication are the role modeling everybody needs.

Young children are learning to use language to express their feelings. Feel free to help them by offering opportunities to do this. When telling a story, ask them how they think a character felt. If no one supplies an answer, offer some possibilities—"Do you think Moses felt angry? Happy?" We are always modeling how to use language. This also applies to manners. Young children are trying to learn how to use language in a polite, kind way. We need to be role models of kind and mannerly interactions.

Parents

Providing a specific role, a meaningful experience, and a spiritual connection with parents may be the most challenging part of any Tot Shabbat program. In almost every other part of adults' lives, they know what their role is, what training it takes to get there, what the social expectations may be, and how to find their way to competence and achievement. Here, the definitions are cloudy, and for some, childhood memories of negative synagogue experiences color their perceptions as they walk through the doors of the synagogue with their children. They may know deep in their hearts "why" they are there, but they aren't quite sure they can trust this set of people and community because of their own baggage.

There is a significant element of intimidation as well. Some parents at Tot Shabbat are fearful they will be called upon and not know the answer. They are successful and confident corporate CEOs, journalists, directors, shopkeepers, therapists, physicians, attorneys, financial wizards, engineers, professors during the week, but they feel inarticulate, inadequate, ignorant, and insecure in their knowledge when they find themselves in a Jewish setting. Some go on automatic pilot to avoid any chance of getting themselves into any circumstance of looking incompetent. They talk, they socialize, they disconnect before they even have a chance to connect. They don't necessarily realize what they are doing, but it is a knee-jerk reaction to such an incredibly uncomfortable situation. Think of the class clowns in religious school classes. Sure they need attention, sure they may be talented and good entertainers, but they may also be avoiding that which is difficult and painful for them to face—the actual learning of the material.

How do we eliminate these behaviors and turn parents into productive participants and models for their children? By building relationships. Parents must be encouraged to sit with their children and participate, and they must never be made to feel judged. If parents are accepted for where they are (just like the children), they will grow to feel more and more comfortable at Tot Shabbat. This will create a wonderful opportunity to connect, establish, and grow trust. Parents need positive, warm synagogue experiences in the synagogue, and if they can have these experiences with their children, even better!

There are many wonderful, creative, motivated, and skilled parents waiting to be asked to become an integral part of the Tot Shabbat experience. There are several "successful" Tot Shabbat programs around the country that are in fact lay led. These capable adults can take on roles ranging from puppeteering to carpentry to building a special Tot Shabbat *Aron HaKodesh* (ark); they can be artists who help families create meaningful, long-lasting ritual objects. The potential is boundless, but the recruitment starts with the development of trusting relationships.

Each institution must experiment and create a recipe that works for them according to their own circumstances. The culture of the community, the history of the program, the relationships among senior staff, the interplay between lay leadership and senior staff, the flexibility of the facility, and the backgrounds from which these families with young children are coming are just a few of the puzzle pieces that must be considered in planning.

Siblings

It's very important to be aware of and recognize the children who are older than five at the Tot Shabbat. They may be there because the whole family is there, but the style of the service may not resonate for them. If there are one or two, or a small group of five or six, special roles can be identified for them that give them a position of *kavod* (honor) and meaning. This gives them meaning and purpose in an environment that doesn't really recognize them otherwise, and it provides the younger children with an opportunity to see the older children in leadership roles.

If there is a routine to their attendance, then you have the opportunity of planning with them and even bringing them into the planning process. What are their strengths or talents? Can they participate musically with their guitar or violin? Can they prepare a two-minute role-play of the Torah portion? Can they be in charge of taking out the Torah and leading the *hakafah*? They enjoy feeling like the "big kids" everyone looks up to and can be contributing members of the Tot Shabbat community.

Conclusion

Tot Shabbat can play a powerful role in a congregation's healthy ritual life, diverse education system, and forward-thinking membership strategy. While planning Tot Shabbat, it is important to ask the following questions: What happens at the next stages of growth for which you are preparing these children? Where are the adults in their own religious lives, and where would we like them to move to? What kinds of experiences will help both children and adults to grow and be open to new Jewish and spiritual experiences? What role can the leader play in helping them create wonderful Jewish memories they will have for the rest of their lives? The memories these families create today will have an enormous influence on their future (Jewish) life decisions.

While the responsibilities are great and may at times seem overwhelming, the rewards of Tot Shabbat are beyond measure. How many other congregants will run up to you with a hug and a kiss? How many other congregants will, when they see you, turn a frown into a big toothless smile? How many other congregants will watch you wide-eyed with wonder? There is no greater feeling than knowing that you are helping families be Jewish families. This is holy work.

Part III

How Do We Create a Successful Tot Shabbat?

6

Connecting Young Children and Their Families to Prayer and Torah

Treasure L. Cohen

Today, when many congregations are practically bursting with young families, it is hard to remember that not long ago little children were practically invisible in synagogues. Back then, conventional wisdom held that young children and synagogue services were basically incompatible. The standard religious service was high on decorum and low on active participation; young children, on the other hand, were low in decorum and high in activity, distraction, and disruption. Although some children could sit passively and obediently and others would run wild in the halls, most young Jewish children never stepped foot in a synagogue, except perhaps on Purim or Simchat Torah, and more significantly, neither did their parents.

A generation ago, my husband and I were part of a tiny minority of young parents at Congregation Beth El in South Orange, New Jersey, who saw Shabbat attendance as part of their weekly rhythm and wanted to share this experience with their children. On good days, it was a joy to bring our children to services—watching their faces light up when it was time to kiss the Torah, bouncing them on our laps to the traditional melodies, or hearing them belt out *Adon Olam* without inhibition. On other days, we wondered why we had come at all, as we stood vigil in the synagogue lobby with our small children, priming them with books, toys, and nibbles and shushing them to avoid the disapproval of our fellow congregants. We wanted to be part of the Shabbat community, but there was no place for nursing babies, needy toddlers, or exuberant preschoolers—or their parents.

But times were changing. In the era before "Torah-for-Tots," when parents were expecting more of their institutions (synagogues included) and first-generation Sesame Streeters were proving how crucial early education was, we introduced a new kind of worship service at our synagogue community: Shabbat and High Holy Day Services for Young Families. As parents and teachers, we wanted to provide exciting and enriching early experiences for our children; we wanted our children to share a love and connection to prayer, Torah, spirituality, and community; and we wanted to be involved in the transmission of Jewish tradition from generation to generation.

Thirty years later, we are still leading services for young children—no longer for our own children, but for cascading generations of children and their families. The service has evolved, as have we as service leaders. We have watched children and their parents begin their Jewish journey with us and continue to grow and flourish as Jewish learners and leaders. And in the process, we have learned a lot about how young children connect to prayer, Torah, spirituality, and community.

Young Children and Prayer

In constructing the traditional service, the Rabbis had an astute understanding of human nature. Every service included a warm-up, movement and choreography, ritual and routine coupled with new learning, and solitary meditation coupled with communal celebration. The young family services offered at my synagogue follow the same rhythm and order, adapted to fit the needs and attention span of young children. We begin every service with warm-up songs and then proceed to the liturgy familiar to congregants from the main service. Our service includes a Torah parade and a new story or *parashah* every week. We offer an opportunity for personal prayer and an opportunity for communal celebration. And of course, it would not be true to our tradition if we did not end with *Kiddush*, food, and socializing.

At first, we chose not to use a siddur (prayer book), not only because most young children cannot read, but also because we did not want the written page to come between the children (and adults) and their true expression of prayer. Instead we concentrated on building a familiarity with the "oral" tradition—connecting the children to the songs, words, and rhythms of prayer through clapping, singing, and dancing. Next we focused on creating a connection between the Hebrew words and the essence of the prayer. Inspired by Rabbi Dan Grossman, a teacher and user of sign language in worship, we added a vocabulary of Jewish signs to match key words in the prayer liturgy. Each sign became a bridge to meaning, requiring no English translation. The signs also served to connect the many grammatical Hebrew variations of one word with its essence. *baruch*, *b'rachah*, and *Bar'chu* all had the same sign for "blessing." In time, we developed a whole prayer vocabulary with corresponding signs. For the children, this exercised their auditory skills and gave them an opportunity for active prayer. For children and adults alike, the signing and movement became a kind of poetry in motion.

Movement is so embedded in Jewish prayer that the sign for davening (praying) involves *shuckeling*, a rocking back-and-forth motion. Traditional prayer has an assigned choreography: we bow at the *Bar'chu*; we rise on our tiptoes during the *K'dushah*; we parade the Torah before and after the Torah reading.

How well this fits in with the natural body movements of young children who are practically never still! In our service, we incorporate these movements into the prayer experience, never in a subtle way. When we bow during the *Bar'chu*, we also sweep our arms from the upward position of receiving blessings to the outward position of sharing blessings. Instead of simply rising on our toes during the *K'dushah*, we jump up three times, as we try to be kinder, better, and more holy.

As the service evolved, we added a visual component. In an era when "Big Books" were taking over the classroom, I developed a "Big Book Siddur," which became a centerpiece for communal prayer. Each large page was illustrated to represent a prayer, and each prayer had one word associated with it. Some pages were interactive: the *Bar'chu* had two people "bowing" at the waist (compliments of a paper fastener); the *Amidah* had two people standing up (emerging out of a library pocket.) The words, written on white tagboard and housed in clear plastic sheet covers, were removable. Each prayer had a (child) leader who held up the written word every time the spoken word was uttered. Quite miraculously, the children began to "read" and identify the Hebrew words.

When parents tell me that their children sing "Shabbat Shalom" in the bathtub or that *V'shamru* is their favorite song, I am always happy. But when they tell me that they can hardly wait to get to services to share their *Shehecheyanus*, I know that I have done my job. I believe that for young children and their parents, prayer must be more than words and music and choreography, even though that is the language of transmission. If it is going to take on lifetime importance, it must have a personal value. We must give children an opportunity to build a relationship with God.

I have also discovered that children, beginning at age three, are not only capable of cultivating a relationship with God, but that this relationship satisfies a very basic developmental need for security and protection. In an adult service, there are many opportunities for daveners to talk to God through the language of prayer—whether thanking, petitioning, or pouring out their hearts. In our children's services, we try to provide similar opportunities for young children. During the *Amidah*, we give children private time to talk to God, suggesting that they close their eyes and giving them the following guidance:

> Now is the time to share with God something that is making you happy or something that is making you sad. Something that is making you excited or something that is making you worried. We'll know you are done with your private prayer when you are sitting down and your eyes are open.

It is amazing to look out on the congregation and see children deep in concentration and watching them take their seats at different times.

Most parents will tell you that one of their goals for their young children is to teach them to say "Thank you"—a value that is entirely compatible with our Jewish tradition, which challenges us to say one hundred blessings a day. We know that children love to celebrate, and most classrooms give children time to share their triumphs and acquisitions through that age-old institution "Show and Tell." In our children's service, "Show and Tell" is transformed into "*Shehecheyanus.*" Right before the Torah service, children can come forward and share their milestone of the week, whether it's losing a tooth, performing a mitzvah (like cleaning up their room), or, the *Shehecheyanu* of *Shehecheyanus*, their birthday. When every child has had an opportunity to share their personal *Shehecheyanu* with the congregation, there is a communal *Shehecheyanu* blessing and dance. In their tenure at children's services, we have watched children go from learning to walk, to becoming toilet trained, to losing a tooth, to riding a bike—and we have all celebrated these milestones together.

Young Children and Torah

If the prayer service provides the comfort and predictability of ritual, the Torah reading contributes the element of new learning and spiritual growth to every service. Not only do we read a new "story" every week, but we introduce it with the spectacle of a Torah procession, which captivates us visually and musically and also creates the intimacy that allows the congregation to touch and kiss the Torah and to greet each other. An early childhood specialist could not have created a better model for engaging young and old alike in the excitement and connection to Torah!

Every children's service includes a Torah service and parade. There are enough small Torahs—miniature, stuffed, velvet-cloaked—that every child gets to hold a Torah in the procession. The biggest Torah—a life-sized but stuffed Torah—goes to the birthday or special-*simchah* child, who leads the others around the room as we sing "Am Yisrael Chai." From the youngest to the oldest, children participate in this parade—singing, dancing, moving, and embracing the Torah.

What follows is the Torah "story." Children sit in front of the ark, "Torah-sitting" and cuddling their small Torahs. On Shabbat morning, the Torah story is told from a picture Torah scroll that has been drawn on a roll of shelf paper and laminated. Each week, the children hear and see an episode of the Torah saga, which follows the narrative more than the *parashah*. Through the weekly story, they are introduced to the characters, concepts, and values that are central to our Jewish tradition. What makes it even more exciting is that each week we leave off at a pivotal point in the story and remind them to come back next week to hear what happened next.

Being the "Torah-teller" requires preparation. First, it is necessary to read the Torah story in its original form, then to shape it so that a young child can connect to its content and meaning in a developmental way. Every story contains names, personalities, issues, and conflicts that young children can identify with. Children can understand Adam and Eve because they know that when they really want something, it is very hard to have self-control. When we talk about Noah's ark or the Golden Calf, we can bring in the challenge of patience and having to wait. When Abraham or Rebecca must journey to a new land, we can focus on how hard it is to separate. As we read the Torah narrative, we discover how many of the struggles of the early Jewish people resemble the same struggles, conflicts, and challenges of young children.

The Family Experience

Above and beyond everything else, one of the most powerful things about the young family service is watching parent and child bond in the shared experience of prayer and Torah. In a world in which parents are constantly in motion, it provides children with a rare opportunity to sit and snuggle in their parents' laps and to associate a Jewish learning experience with the comfort and security of their parents' presence. Having their parents sitting next to them also gives the service a weight and value that indicates it is important and central to their lives. For parents, it is an opportunity to reevaluate and renew their worship experience as they learn and grow alongside their child. So many parents have told me that as a result of sharing Shabbat and holiday services, Torah and God have become part of the family conversation throughout the week.

Watching the interaction between parent and child, I am convinced that this dynamic is an essential ingredient in the development of a positive worship experience for young children. In fact, this "family model" is resonant of a traditional worship experience, where there are no entrance requirements by age, level of education, or background experience. I believe that a service should not be a classroom, where prayer is taught and learners are separated by ability or developmental level. A service is rather a multisensory experience where participants can connect to prayer in their own way and find their own personal path—whether through the music, the Torah, the spirituality, or the community connections.

The Positive Impact of Tot Shabbat through the Years

Over the past thirty years, we have seen generations of families begin their connection to prayer and community at young family services. Children, parents, and grandparents have sung together, danced together, prayed together, and learned together in a joyful and positive setting. We have seen families who once tiptoed tentatively into our services become active in the congregation—as daveners and as community leaders. We have watched children grow from their earliest toddle with a stuffed Torah through their bar/bat mitzvah to their own Jewish community involvement and leadership. Finally, we are seeing those children who once sang and danced and prayed becoming the parents of a new generation of children who are dancing, singing, and praying.

Each generation brings its own challenges. Today's families are more diverse than ever before, with an expanding palate of wishes and needs. For example, since there are so many working parents whose demanding lives drive their schedules, we now begin every Friday night service with a dinner to reduce the hassles and stress in their lives. Babysitters are hired on both Friday night and Shabbat morning to provide support to parents—both before the children's service begins and to help with toddlers during the service. We also now provide Jewish children's book collections in the back of the main sanctuary for children who want to cuddle beside their parents during the traditional service and toys in the social hall behind the main sanctuary for children to play with before the children's service begins and during *Kiddush*. And for me, the biggest change is that we are no longer the only service leaders. There is a corps of new leaders who are bringing their talents and experience to this important mission.

As with other aspects of Jewish communal life, synagogue worship evolves, changes, and grows from generation to generation. Unlike thirty years ago, the doors of the synagogue are now open to new generations of young families, and congregations work to create experiences for young children and their families that are authentically Jewish and compatible with their needs. From our experience, we have found that young family services have been a warm and welcoming gateway, connecting children and their parents to prayer, Torah, and community and creating a foundation for a lifetime of Jewish learning and living. That has become the fulfillment of our hopes and goals. Providing Shabbat and holiday services for young children and their families has been good for the children, good for their parents, good for the synagogue, and good for the Jewish future.

7

Essentials in Conducting Tot Shabbat

Deborah K. Bravo

Leading Tot Shabbat for the first time can be a scary and intimidating experience. It is especially challenging because the leader must be comfortable with very young children as well as adults. For some of us, being comfortable around young children comes naturally, while for others, leading Tot Shabbat crosses our line of comfort. Either way, the knowledge of how to interact with young children can really help anyone lead a successful Tot Shabbat. If you keep some of the principles that follow in mind, you can become a confident Tot Shabbat leader. Children are very forgiving and don't even notice what we might consider to be mistakes. The key is to enjoy the children and the service. So relax, and the children will love the Tot Shabbat experience you provide for them!

Leader's Demeanor

There is no question that much of the success of any Tot Shabbat depends on the presence and demeanor of the Tot Shabbat leader. It is important as the leader to command respect but also to remain flexible and loose. At any given Tot Shabbat, the response from the crowd might be different, so you need to be willing and able to alter your plan and demeanor to meet the needs of the group.

It is important to maintain control at all times while showing the children you can have fun and be relaxed. But never let them take over. I find when I can wear comfortable clothing that enables me to sit on the floor with them or dance around the sanctuary with them, it invites the children to behave in a similar manner.

Many clergy are most comfortable being up on the bimah. I find the Tot Shabbat experience to be much more powerful when I am with the children. As it is, I tower over them, so I make a great effort to be closer to them. I utilize the bimah, especially the ark, during the service, but we all go on the bimah together.

The demeanor of the leader at the beginning of the service is particularly important. It sets the tone for the rest of the service. If the Tot Shabbat begins in an open, welcoming manner, it helps the children and parents to feel more comfortable and at ease. However, the structure is important so that the children can see that there are guidelines to this experience.

I find there are certain tools that help to open my demeanor as a leader, from a cordless microphone that enables me to walk around (if I need a microphone) to egg shakers for the children to use throughout the service. What is most important is to make Tot Shabbat casual and welcoming for the children and their parents. Tot Shabbat is a great time to let your playful side come out. Don't be afraid to be yourself, release your inner child, and let the children enjoy who you are at the soul—on the inside.

Leader's Expression

Tot Shabbat should be an uplifting and exciting experience for all who attend. Similar to the leader's demeanor, the leader's expression, both outward and inward, can largely impact the outcome of the Tot Shabbat experience. The Tot Shabbat experience should always be a positive one for its participants, and that positive experience can result largely from the attitude and expression of the leader.

If the leader chooses to ask a question of the Tot Shabbat participants, it is important to maintain a positive expression with the children. Even if the answer is incorrect (the holiday coming up is Purim, not Chanukah), respond positively ("That's a great answer, but it's not that holiday" or "Wow, I wish it was Chanukah coming up, but that's not it"). Encourage the children to continue to respond and answer your questions, but guide them positively toward correct answers. One excellent technique with children is to ask questions that don't really have "correct" answers. When we ask what they are thankful for, anything goes: the earth, animals, air, sun, and moon, as well as things like Mom, Dad, my brother, my sister, and me! Anything is really OK.

Another way to encourage interaction with the children is to have them mimic what you do. By inviting them to repeat words, phrases, melodies, hand motions, or clapping after you, you create an inviting and engaging atmosphere. Obviously, the expression and attitude of the leader are what the children sense. If the leader is happy to be at Tot Shabbat, the children know that. If the leader would rather be somewhere else or feels it is a waste of his or her time, they sense that as well.

One of the most wonderful characteristics of young children is that they can be so positively influenced by the leader and the mood of the service. A child who enters the room shy, angry, or sad can leave happy, excited, and focused. The younger they are, the quicker their moods can change, which is a great tool for the leader!

Voice Intonation

There are a number of important rules to follow when leading Tot Shabbat experiences, especially regarding the leader's voice. It is important to find your own way to speak with young children that in no way talks down to them. They want to feel important and special, and you need to do that at their level, but in an important and significant manner.

Through the voice of the leader, the group can be calmed or excited. The whisper voice will create one setting, while the excited voice creates a very different yet equally powerful one. However you change your voice, be sure to be joyful, remembering that the celebration of Shabbat is just that—a celebration!

Starting at the beginning of the service, you can easily create different moods using different levels of your voice. When we sing "Hinei Mah Tov," with the children repeating after me, we do it loudly and then softly, and the mood is very different but equally effective both ways. Though we often are spirited, led by me as the leader, I make sure to differentiate between being energetic and screaming.

In every Tot Shabbat experience, you need to find a way to quiet the children down and get their attention and focus. Some people use their voice to do it. It's a great technique. You ask them in a very quiet voice to clap their hands once. Then twice. Then three times. Usually at that point, everyone is captivated, waiting to see what will be next. Be sure you have something to do. Young children can never sit around wondering what will be next. It is very important that you plan carefully so that you flow from one prayer, song, or activity to the next. If there is waiting or dead time, that is when you lose them.

I am always aware of how much young children model after adults. So be sure, as the leader, that the tone you set with your voice is what you want to hear back from them. If you shout, they will. If you sing, they will. If you speak in a big bimah voice, they will as well. Use your voice to capture them, and then keep them captured through the prayers and lessons.

Speaking to Children and Adults

There is no question that Tot Shabbat is meant to be for young children and adults. For many adults, it is the only service they will attend, so we need to speak and therefore teach at several levels. Adults should never be viewed as the chauffeurs for their children. They should be invited participants in the service.

Some leaders like to put all the children together on the floor in the middle of the space. I prefer to keep them in the chairs for much of the service, either next to or in front of their parents, grandparents, or guardians. I find it helps the children to behave better and it keeps the adults focused and participating. This puts parents within an arm's reach of telling their child to listen or participate.

During our Tot Shabbat experience, there are times when the children are participating separately from the adults (e.g., during the dancing of the *Mi Chamochah*, the Torah service, or the story). However, I give adults a specific role during each of these activities so they don't see it as an opportunity to talk with other adults and disengage from the service. During the dancing of *Mi Chamochah*, the adults are invited to continue to clap and sing while the children march around with their tambourines or shakers. During the Torah service, the children come up to the bimah to receive a stuffed Torah and then march through the congregation holding their Torahs high, while the parents sing the *hakafah* songs. During the story, I always try to have a level of moral or values geared toward the children, while simultaneously sharing a lesson appropriate for the adults.

It is very important to engage and teach both the children and the adults. When we discuss the meaning of the prayers, as concrete and simple as my explanations might be, I know the adults are typically learning something as well. When I try to relate a current event during Tot Shabbat, I know the adults are listening to the parallel too. When I remind the children of the weekly Torah portion and how it is connected to the stories that came before it, the adults are very much a part of that conversation.

Though you obviously want to use language that is appropriate and understood by small children, you are also showing the adults how to talk with the children about certain topics. Adults often ask about how to speak to their children about God, and Tot Shabbat can be a wonderful opportunity to model how to have that conversation.

Some adults will be very eager to engage in this worship experience with their children. Other adults will view this time as babysitting or an opportunity to chat with adult friends. From the beginning, or even in the middle as a reminder, be direct with the adults. This isn't babysitting. This is a worship service. And if they want their children to come, learn, and enjoy, then they need to model the same behaviors. Be clear about what you expect from parents and children, but always do it in a kind, welcoming way.

Appropriate Roles

In our congregation, there are many unwritten rules about how to behave during services. During the late adult service, there is one set of rules. During the family service there is another set of rules. During a Shabbat morning service with a bar or bat mitzvah, there might even be another set of rules. But during Tot Shabbat, I try to help the worried parents, grandparents, or guardians let go of the rules and expectations of the more adult services. Tot Shabbat is geared toward young children, so any rules must be developmentally appropriate for this population.

I try to convince parents of restless children not to take them out of the room. Instead, I try to engage them in what we are doing. I establish from the beginning, and reiterate from time to time, the Tot Shabbat rules, but I allow the adults in the room to enforce those rules. My rules are as follows: no going onto the bimah until the Torah service, no throwing things, and no touching other participants.

My role as the leader of the Tot Shabbat experience is to teach the children (and parents) about holy space. At the beginning, we often look at the *ner tamid* and let that be our reminder of the holy space we are dwelling in. If your Tot Shabbat experience takes place in a space that is not a sanctuary, you can always make a *ner tamid* for that space. When the children start to get crazy (and they will), I simply point to the *ner tamid* and remind them of where we are and why that space is different.

How Is Tot Shabbat Different?

There are a number of aspects of Tot Shabbat that make it different from every other Shabbat experience. First, and perhaps most important, is the timing. If Tot Shabbat is geared toward children aged six and under (or whatever ages you determine), then you need to respect the attention span of that age group.

I have always aimed for a Tot Shabbat to be thirty minutes in length. I always begin promptly, so as not to disadvantage those children who arrived on time and have been sitting already. I like to couple the Tot Shabbat service experience with an activity or a meal, which can obviously make the program go longer, but the service length needs to be appropriate for the advertised ages of the participants.

Young children learn through their senses, and they need to move their bodies. During Tot Shabbat, it is important to create opportunities for children to get up and move around. They can dance, they can sing both sitting and standing, they can make hand motions, they can march, and they can act out a story. It is important for every Tot Shabbat service to include several movement opportunities.

It is important that Tot Shabbat is fully participatory. This is not the time for the clergy or leader to expound for five or ten minutes about the lesson of the week. It needs to be interactive and invite participation. If you are talking "at" your congregation, the children will let you know—you will quickly lose control of the room.

Repetition is a wonderful tool during Tot Shabbat. This is a way you can have pre-readers (typically the majority of the crowd) participate fully. Young children love repetition (how many times do they like to read the same book over and over again?). You may be sick of doing the same songs and routine, but this routine is very important and grounding for young children. Try including some readings that are echo readings, where you as the leader say one line and they repeat it back to you.

It is important during Tot Shabbat to ask of the participants only what you think is within their reach. For example, having children sit through a three-minute silent prayer is not realistic. Adults can barely accomplish that task. But describing the importance of sharing words and thoughts just between them and God, and then inviting them to close their eyes, not to be silly, and just to talk to God, for twenty or thirty seconds, is very achievable.

Prayer books are an interesting dilemma for Tot Shabbat. Some congregations like to have them, at least for the adults. I have found them to be a distraction. The children want to follow, but they can't, and then they don't participate. I like to distribute printed prayers or song sheets for parents when necessary, but I invite the children to simply watch and listen. The other advantage to not having books or song sheets is that the participants' hands are free to clap, move, play instruments, or participate in any physical way they want.

Music, of course, is a crucial element to the Tot Shabbat experience. Familiar songs and catchy tunes are the best way to get children and parents engaged in the Shabbat experience. Music is often the framework for the Tot Shabbat service, and while the words you say change each week, the songs, for the most part, remain the same. Even if you are sick of the "same songs," routine is very important to young children, especially if they are only coming about once a month.

How to Lead and Teach Prayers on a Young Child's Level

It is important to be practical and realistic when setting your goals for the Tot Shabbat service. Of course, as the leader, you will want to help the children to grow and learn, but remember that sometimes the basic information, basic facts, and basic explanations are far more appropriate and will last a lot longer than the complicated ones. Stick to the concrete as much as possible, as this is what young children can understand. Try to keep vocabulary simple. This might mean really thinking through a story or explanation of something to make sure that it is developmentally appropriate for the children.

As a leader, you want them to learn and to retain the information they are learning. And while you want to be concrete and simple, you also don't want to underestimate what the children have the ability to learn. I tend to check in with them from week to week, or month to month, and when they are able to recall what we did the prior time, then we move on to a deeper level of understanding. The key is to keep your Tot Shabbat accessible to newcomers while offering new learning and growth to your regulars. If you are open, playful, and flexible, you and your families will have a wonderful Tot Shabbat experience!

8

God's Spirit Is in the Details

Paula Feldstein and Jordan Millstein

When Paula was a child, her piano teacher told her that learning to play the piano would be 10 percent inspiration and 90 percent perspiration. Her mother later told her that this was true of marriage as well—some wisdom that has served us well. This is also true of planning a successful Tot Shabbat. One should never underestimate the importance of advance planning and logistics when it comes to Tot Shabbat. The ideal Tot Shabbat service is a successful experience for everyone. The leader succeeds when he or she can connect with the families and hold almost everyone's attention (it's hard to get 100 percent) without standing on his or her head. The parents succeed when they feel comfortable, are engaged, and are able to pray and breathe a little because their children are engaged. The children succeed when they are able to sing, pray, move their bodies, learn, and grow without being constantly "shushed" by the adults in the room.

Following are some of the logistical issues we think about when we plan a Tot Shabbat service.

Holy Space

There are many schools of thought when it comes to where Tot Shabbat should be held. Many leaders like to hold the entire service on the bimah in the sanctuary. The benefits of being in the sanctuary are significant. It gives young children the experience of being in the space that the community considers holy. There are many meaningful ritual items to see and learn about—the ark, the Torah, the *ner tamid* (eternal light). As the service leader, it gives you the opportunity to teach the children what it means to be in a sanctuary and the proper way to behave when we are there. In some congregations, depending on the layout of the bimah and the number of children who attend, this may work well.

But it might also cause problems. The first thing to consider when looking at a space for Tot Shabbat is what in the space may distract the children. If you hold Tot Shabbat in a classroom and there are toys in the room, unless they are hidden, you are in big trouble. The bimah might be nice if the children can

51

sit on it with plenty of elbow room and nothing else to distract them. If, however, they are crowded up there, they will be have trouble keeping their hands to themselves, and if some of them are on or near the stairs, climbing up and down the stairs might be more interesting than anything you are trying to engage them in. It is also important that children sit with parents, for a variety of reasons, which we will discuss later. If there is only enough room on the bimah for children without parents, you may find yourself leading a service with no parental help, interaction, or engagement. Parents often end up schmoozing with each other, which can also become disruptive. There may be a time in the service when you want to bring the children up on the bimah for a short time (during a Torah reading or to march around with the Torah), but having them separated from their parents for any extended period is asking for trouble. Thus, while the sanctuary is certainly a holy space, and it is important to teach the children about what is in the sanctuary and why it is holy, it may not be the best space for your Tot Shabbat.

We have done Tot Shabbat in classrooms (with the toys hidden) and in multipurpose rooms with a portable ark. Having the ark and the Torah nearby are important, but so is having a space where parents can sit with children, children have room to move their bodies without hitting each other, there are few distractions from the task at hand, and everyone can be as close to the leader as possible. Our ideal space has chairs where children can sit with parents for the majority of the service but also a floor space for children to come up close for a story or Torah reading. It also helps children if they can move around during the course of the service. Another thing to consider in creating holy space is sound. The *Sh'ma* says, "Hear, O Israel!" But will they be able to hear? The size of the room, the strength of your voice, and the musical instruments you may use are all factors in determining what kind of sound system may be necessary. Just because you may be used to leading other groups of similar size or in a similar space does not mean you will not need a microphone at an active, joyous (read: loud) Tot Shabbat!

Holy Time

In order to have a successful Tot Shabbat, the time and length of the service must reflect what is developmentally appropriate for young children. There is no one "perfect" time to hold the service, but congregations seem to have the greatest success with either an early Friday night service or a relatively early Saturday morning service. Since many young children go to bed by 7:00 or 7:30, most congregations hold their Friday night Tot Shabbat at around 6:00 p.m. This can be challenging for parents coming home from work, but if there is a Shabbat dinner afterwards, this allows parents to come straight from work without having to worry about what to make for dinner, and it also gives families time to socialize after the service, building community. On Shabbat morning, Tot Shabbat is usually held fairly early (since young children get up early and many of them need to nap), around 9:00 a.m. When we served Temple Emanuel in Worcester, Massachusetts, the Tot Shabbat service was held at 9:30 a.m., followed by a *Kiddush* and all kinds of activities that lasted until about 11:30 a.m. This way, families could come for Tot Shabbat and stay as long as they wanted, depending on naps and other family needs. Many stayed for the whole morning and had a lot of time to socialize.

How long a Tot Shabbat service should last is a very important question. Young children have limited attention spans. When we ask them to be engaged for too long, we are setting unrealistic expectations and setting up them (and us) for failure. The typical Tot Shabbat we lead runs about thirty minutes, although we have stretched it to forty when everything is going well and when children are on the older side (aged four or five, as opposed to two or three). The key here is flexibility. It is important to plan thoroughly but be willing to adjust the plan when necessary. It does not matter how many more songs or prayers you have in your plan, if you are losing the focus of the children, it may be time to go directly to the closing song. One year, we were leading a Tot Rosh HaShanah service at North Shore Congregation Israel in Glencoe, Illinois. There were about four hundred people there—a tough crowd to keep focused under the best of circumstances! The congregation was facing a wall that was all windows, and behind the windows was a big lawn. About twenty-five minutes into the service I suddenly noticed that there were several deer walking across the lawn. It was clear that if the children saw the deer, they would go running to the windows, and there would be no way to get them back to their seats and focus on the service. We immediately announced our concluding song. By the time it ended, we were singing *"L'shanah tovah tikateivu"* to the deer on the lawn. No matter what you have planned and how engaging it is, when the children have reached the end of their attention spans, it is time to quit. That way the service ends and everyone feels that it was a good experience.

Holy Words

There is some debate among those who lead Tot Shabbat about whether to use a siddur (prayer book). On the one hand, it is wonderful for children to hold a holy book in their hands and know that it is special (just as the grown-ups do). A young children's siddur with engaging and appropriate pictures and with words for the adults can be a useful tool. The problem with a siddur is that it does not leave the children's hands free to clap or move. Treasure Cohen and other Tot Shabbat leaders have a solution for this problem: create one large siddur that is put in front of the congregation. It has pictures and simple language and allows the adults' and children's hands to be free. Recently, some congregations have begun to use large monitors or screens on which the prayers or songs are projected. Then there is another school of thought that says that children this age do not need a siddur at all. Marilyn Price calls this the "hands-free service." The advantage of this approach is that the adults and children are able to participate in the service with their whole bodies and souls and engage fully with the leader without anything else to pay attention to. Some congregations hand out song sheets for the adults so that they will have the words to the prayers. However, some argue that if there are so many words that the adults need song sheets, there are too many words for the young children to sing and learn.

Wholly Engaged

One of the issues with which many Tot Shabbat leaders struggle is what to do when parents stand in the back of the room schmoozing instead of sitting and engaging with their children. This is particularly delicate because it is the job of the leader to set the tone and the rules so that the Tot Shabbat can succeed. However, it is also the job of the leader to be warm and welcoming and not make anyone feel singled out, embarrassed, or put out. One of the best ideas for how to handle this was shared by Treasure Cohen. When she leads a Tot Shabbat service, Treasure talks about how in this busy, busy world, parents' laps are always in motion—never in one place for very long. Tot Shabbat is a chance for parents' laps to be still and for children to be in them. She explains to the parents that she wants them to sit with their children, not necessarily to keep them under control, but because cuddling and snuggling are an important part of Tot Shabbat. She asks the participants, "Can you reach out and touch your child? Can you reach out and touch your grown-up?" When we used this technique, followed by everyone sharing a big Shabbat hug, it was very successful in getting the families to sit together and started Shabbat off in a loving, warm, and affectionate way. Many ways to engage adults and children can be found in this book. Part of this engagement is finding ways to get family members to interact with one another as well as ways to get families to interact with other families. These are all things to consider when planning a service.

Holy Cow!

Many Tot Shabbat leaders have some sort of "shtick" they use. We like to use puppets, including a cow puppet named Rabbi Holstein who wears a tallit and *kippah* and speaks like Bullwinkle. There are many types of shtick: a puppet, a song that gets a little silly, special hand motions or props. These techniques can be extremely effective if they serve the goals of the service. The goal of Tot Shabbat is to create a worship experience for young children and their families. There are many goals that fall under this: learning prayers, talking about God, sharing blessings and sorrows, and so on. What is most important is that the goals are always clear in the leader's mind and that the shtick serves the goals rather than the other way around. The silly puppet who does not know what Shabbat is can be a very effective tool for teaching about Shabbat. Shtick becomes problematic, however, when it becomes the center of the action and not a means for teaching something. If there is no clear reason for bringing the puppet out, don't use the puppet. Planning Tot Shabbat is like writing a well-crafted lesson plan: everything must be there to accomplish the goals.

Holy Teaching

Tot Shabbat is worship but it is also like a learners' minyan. It is an opportunity to teach not only children about prayer and God but adults as well. We cannot assume participants have any knowledge of Judaism or prayer vocabulary. Do not assume that the participants know the answers to the following questions:

What does it mean to pray? Where is God? What do we want to thank God for? Young children are concrete thinkers with an incredible openness and natural curiosity. They are natural theologians. Don't be afraid to interrupt the flow of prayer to talk about prayer. Be sure to ask questions, encourage everyone's ideas and answers, and then quickly return to singing and moving.

Holy Rituals

Having a set routine is an important part of maintaining an effective ritual. Young children love routine (how many times do they like to hear the same bedtime story over and over again?). There is actual brain research showing that routine and rituals are comforting to people because they soothe the brain stem. Not surprisingly, consistency in the way we lead Tot Shabbat is important. A consistent routine is even more important because most congregations only hold Tot Shabbat about once a month. For young children a month is a very long time, and they forget much of what they learn from one Tot Shabbat to the next. If you are lucky, you will also have new families coming each time, and they need to learn. While your story and some of your teaching might change, we advise keeping the core service and music the same from month to month. We do not use a siddur in our Tot Shabbat services, but we do have a *seder*, a clear order. This will help the participants become comfortable and attached to the prayers and songs.

Creating an effective service also involves developing a smooth flow from one action or ritual to the next. One of the reasons it is important to plan so carefully for Tot Shabbat is that it is crucial to maintain consistent flow and a rapid pace. Young children do not sit patiently while we figure out what comes next. The service needs to move smoothly (really any service should) from one prayer to the next and from one part of the service to the next without breaks or long pauses. It is easy to lose the group and hard to get everyone's focus back again. Be flexible. If something is not working (e.g., if no one is answering your questions about something), quickly cut your losses and move on. If you are doing a story with puppets or props (always fun to do), make sure you have everything organized and within easy reach. If you pause to find something or set something up, you will lose the group and have to regain their attention. If you have a large group for Tot Shabbat, it is easier to lead with another person so that one person can always keep things moving (e.g., one can be leading a song while the other is getting out the props for the story).

Holy Feeling

Once you have planned and thought through all the logistics of your Tot Shabbat, the most important thing you can do is enjoy. Look out at the faces of the children as they sing and move to the prayers. Soak in the joy of parents as they cuddle with their children. Don't be afraid to let your inner child loose a bit. Laugh at the adorable things the children say, and encourage the profound things they say. Enjoy the singing, the movement, and the joy of celebrating Shabbat. Your joy and pleasure will be contagious. Allow yourself to feel the spiritual moments that you are helping to create for our youngest Jewish families, and know that you are helping them make wonderful memories and connections as they start their Jewish journeys.

Tot Shabbat Setup Checklist

1. **Publicity:** Publicize your Tot Shabbat through any and every avenue possible. Think about where young families are likely to go, and post flyers there (e.g., the JCC, early childhood centers, libraries, local bookstores, supermarkets). If you are not the early childhood center (ECC) director but have an ECC in your synagogue, make sure the ECC director and teachers are including Tot Shabbat in their mailings and consistently talking it up. Make phone calls. Send e-mails. Don't assume "They all know." Be sure to define who the service is for; not everyone knows what Tot Shabbat is or who should participate. If you want older siblings to feel welcome, be sure to say so.

2. **Participants:** Invite a few families to have a specific role in your Tot Shabbat each month. Then you know you have at least a few families coming. Also, if you have an early childhood center, send a special note home to all the children who have birthdays that month, inviting them to come for their birthday blessing.

3. **Greeters:** Ask a family you know to come a few minutes early, stand by the door, and wish everyone who arrives a *Shabbat shalom*. If someone new comes, have the greeters introduce them to you and others.

4. **Lay leadership:** Invite an officer of your congregation and/or members of the membership committee to come and welcome any new families. When an officer of the congregation stands up and offers words of welcome (keep it brief), it shows the participants that this service is important to the congregation.

5. *Oneg Shabbat*: Make sure that an *Oneg Shabbat* will be set up with age-appropriate drinks and snacks.

6. **Physical space:** Think about which room you will use and how you want the space arranged. Do you want enough chairs for everyone present? Do you want open floor space for the children to sit together for a story? Try to set up the chairs in a way that will encourage everyone to be as close together and as close to the front as possible. If you are not in the sanctuary, what might you need? An ark? An eternal light? *Kippot*? Candles, wine, and challah? A guitar and/or guitar stand? A music stand?

7. **Sound system:** Will you use a sound system? On the one hand, microphones and their cords can be awkward. On the other hand, straining your voice is never a good idea. Children love to participate by sharing their ideas and answers into the microphone. Having a cordless microphone that you can share or a microphone with a very long cord is helpful.

8. **Siddurim and song sheets:** If you are going to use prayer books or song sheets, those obviously have to be available. We suggest designating a family to act as ushers and hand these out.

9. **Props:** If you are going to use puppets or props for your story, make sure you not only have them with you but that they are organized in such a way that you can grab them quickly. If you have to stop to organize yourself for the story, you will lose the room. Having said that, it's good to keep props put away (in a bag or box) during the rest of the service so that they don't become a distraction. Also, if you are going to use egg shakers or little musical instruments, it is best to keep them out of sight except when you want to use them. They are both distracting and noisy!

10. **Service leaders:** Who will lead the service? One person can certainly lead Tot Shabbat, but sometimes having an extra set of hands is very helpful.

Whatever the specific arrangements are, a well-planned Tot Shabbat will help the flow and alleviate a lot of stress. Advance planning will allow the leader to be in the moment and really enjoy the spirit of Tot Shabbat!

9

Involving Parents in Leadership and Planning

Shawna Brynjegard-Bialik

While it may seem counterintuitive to suggest that adding another committee meeting to your already busy schedule will be beneficial, a Tot Shabbat parent committee can be an asset to your synagogue. Opening up leadership of Tot Shabbat to a parent committee gives both parents and the program a chance to grow, and it's not hard to get started. The Tot Shabbat committee should seem like the easiest committee to serve on. You want parents to be thinking, "I already go to Tot Shabbat; how can I help out?"

Parent involvement benefits the program in that it can lead to better planning and more unique activities. Encouraging such involvement brings its own challenges, of course. One must attract the interest of the parents, help them to form a committee, and then provide the committee with enough direction to ensure successful programs and enough freedom to empower the parents to make their own decisions about Tot Shabbat. Parents can do everything for Tot Shabbat, and taking advantage of that can be beneficial to you and your program.

Benefits of Parent Involvement

Involving laypeople can even improve an already great program as well as jumpstart a struggling one. Parents can provide a perspective, energy, and ideas that will enrich your programs. Usually the Tot Shabbat committee does not plan the service. The committee instead plans and sets up the other aspects of Tot Shabbat: the activities and crafts, the snacks, the theme. They do not tell the leader (rabbi, cantor, educator, or layperson) what to read or which prayers to say, which makes for a much simpler arrangement.

Each year has the potential to add new parents to the committee and new activities to the program. Parents bring a diverse set of skills to Tot Shabbat. There are dads who are artistic, moms who excel at organization, parents who know advertising, and couples whose social network draws people in. Ideally, you should not be dramatically changing the format from year to year, but rather bringing in new ideas and projects based on the talents of the parents to keep it fresh. One year you may have more cooking projects and another year you may have more keepsake crafts, depending on the talents and interests of the parents involved.

Parents also bring with them ideas from a wide pool of sources. Moms talk to other moms who belong to other synagogues and schools; dads do the same. These parents will bring ideas for activities they have heard about elsewhere, and in turn, news about what is being done at your Tot Shabbat will be shared as well. Ultimately, involvement on the Tot Shabbat committee can be a gateway to serving on other early childhood or synagogue committees, increasing parent participation beyond the Tot Shabbat years.

If you find that attendance at Tot Shabbat is sparse, involving parents might help you find a solution. Involving parents helps you figure out how to adjust the scheduling of your activities, or—even better—with parents invested in the success of Tot Shabbat, they are more likely to schedule other activities around Tot Shabbat. And let's not forget that at its most basic level, parents on the Tot Shabbat committee will attend Tot Shabbat with their families and invite their friends to go, so program participation will increase.

Recruiting Parents

When forming a Tot Shabbat committee, the most important thing to remember is that the committee members will be the parents of young children. What does this mean? The Tot Shabbat committee has to be convenient for parents of young children. Fortunately, we already know the easiest way to make the Tot Shabbat committee convenient for parents: have only one meeting. This has the added benefit of making it easy for the director or clergy as well. Before you can have an annual meeting, first you need to find parents who are interested in Tot Shabbat. And if there aren't any, you need to get parents interested.

To be successful in recruiting new committee members, start by removing barriers to parent participation. Tot Shabbat can seem intimidating to young families. Parents may feel that while they have a good grasp of the "tot" aspect, they can be less confident about the "Shabbat" part. The Tot Shabbat committee sounds like a religious practice committee, and that can leave parents thinking that only the more observant members can join.

Let parents know that they do not need to be experts in Shabbat observance, that enthusiasm and ideas and a willingness to participate in the committee are all that they need. You want to be clear that no experience is required. In fact, there's really nothing that's required except interest in Tot Shabbat. Remember that parents are often learning about Shabbat right alongside their children and can be embarrassed by their lack of knowledge. Don't let lack of knowledge be a barrier to participation; make it clear that the only prerequisite is having a young child. This is especially true of interfaith families, where a non-Jewish mom who is otherwise very involved in the school might be afraid to participate in Tot Shabbat. Participation in Tot Shabbat and on the Tot Shabbat committee can be a step on the path to increasing Jewish observance; Tot Shabbat is a safe place to learn about Shabbat. Keep in mind that parents should not (unless they are the leader of the service) be asked to plan the service; they are planning the other aspects of the event.

If your early childhood program uses a volunteer interest list for parents to fill out, start your search for committee members by contacting the parents who expressed an interest in Tot Shabbat. You can expand that search by contacting parents of young children who expressed interest in any religious category—for example, holiday celebrations like the Chanukah party, Purim carnival, or Passover model seder.

Another source of committee members is parents who already come to Tot Shabbat. It is easier to recruit parents who are already attending Tot Shabbat because they already know what happens at Tot Shabbat and have an easier time seeing themselves as part of the planning committee. The sense that "I am already here every month anyway" makes Tot Shabbat seem like an easy committee to serve on. Recruiting parents in pairs also helps alleviate the pressure of being on a committee. When there are more people on the committee, there is less pressure to be at every single Tot Shabbat, and if you can get two parents who are already friends, they may view committee participation as another way to socialize. In addition to having a friend to work with, there is also the knowledge that someone else will be helping. A committee with more members provides the potential to rotate responsibilities; it's often easier for busy parents to commit to a whole year when they know that if something comes up, someone else will be there to pick up the slack.

If possible, try to get parents of children of varying ages. If all the committee members are parents of kids set for graduation to an older family or adult service, you will have to start over every year. Try to have a parent or two who will be around for two years or more so there is some sense of continuity and a sense of achievement about growing the program.

Forming a Committee

Once you have anywhere from two to six parents interested in the Tot Shabbat committee, you now need to get them started. The committee should not be too time-intensive; parents are going to be less likely to sign up for something that has weekly meetings (this is true of any committee). My experience at Temple Ahavat Shalom in Northridge, California, was that the Tot Shabbat committee was one of the easiest time commitments. We had one meeting at the beginning of the year where we planned out the whole year of activities. Once everything was planned, the actual work could be handled on our own time or planned further at Tot Shabbat. That initial meeting was always convenient to attend; if school was in session, it was made clear that younger siblings could tag along for the meeting. If school was not in session, child care was provided, making it easier for parents to be there. In addition, a single meeting makes it easier for working parents to participate; if they have to attend only one meeting, it is easier to make it a priority. Of course, because it is a Jewish organization, you can't have a meeting without food.

Parents liked the idea of having only one formal meeting; it proved to be an incentive for participation because you only had to find the time once. In addition, it was understood that with only one meeting it would have to be productive—and it was. A single meeting is also much easier for the rabbi/ educator/early childhood director to attend than yet another series of meetings with yet another committee. A single meeting can give parents a chance to interact with the professional staff at the synagogue, increasing a feeling of connection to the synagogue.

Empowering a Committee

In a single sixty- to ninety-minute meeting you can plan out the whole year of Tot Shabbat. You don't need to reinvent the wheel; if you have a list of activities from previous years, start with that. Make a binder where all Tot Shabbat flyers and calendars are kept so it is easy to see what has been done before. Give parents a chance to talk about what they like and dislike about Tot Shabbat, projects that worked and did not work. For example, we learned from parents that the wood crafts we did one year were a flop: the glue never dried properly, and the projects fell apart in the car on the way home. In September when we sat down to plan the year's activities, more than one parent remembered the mess from the spring before.

Give parents a chance to brainstorm. Even if Tot Shabbat is not new to you, many ideas will be new to them—and contributing to the program is one of the ways parents feel invested. You may expect that at some point each year families will bake challah on Tot Shabbat, but the committee member who suggests baking challah will feel more connected to that month's activity and is more likely to tell friends to attend. Giving parents the power to plan activities gives them a sense of ownership and empowers them to be creative about their own Shabbat observance at home.

When planning for the entire year, it is easier to consider the whole program at once, and not just individual activities out of context; it is easier to see if you are always doing the same type of activity every month, and you are better able to plan a variety of activities and crafts. For example, you'd want to spread out your baking activities (challah, hamantaschen, and matzah). Once you know what you are doing for the year, you can better plan purchasing for the year, combining certain orders to save on shipping costs. This also helps to ensure that you have everything you need and won't be running to the store each month looking for supplies. You can assign committee members a particular month to be in charge; again, it is easier for someone to commit when they know that responsibilities rotate from member to member. And if the year is planned in advance, parents with full-time jobs may be more likely to get involved in planning and participation.

You need to be aware of what the committee members can do—working parents, stay-at-home parents, parents with babies, and parents with older kids all have different time constraints. Remember that they are volunteers and the goal is to empower them, not to overburden them. When you make Tot Shabbat an easy committee to serve on, you get more parents willing to help. Use the committee to help you; if having parents order supplies creates more paperwork for you in reimbursement forms, don't assign parents to do it. Ideally, the committee will be helping the rabbi or education director by taking on some of the responsibility; use them effectively.

Committee Structure

The Tot Shabbat committee should have a chairperson, or co-chairs, as well as a few members. Two members is enough, but you don't need more than five or six.

The chair of the Tot Shabbat committee is the person who works with the early childhood director or the clergyperson who is officially in charge of Tot Shabbat. The chair is responsible for communicating with the committee members, organizing the meeting(s), and reminding committee members about what (if anything) they need to do to prepare for Tot Shabbat. The chair can also be responsible for collecting materials for the committee binder and making notes about what activities should and should not be repeated. At the very least, the chair should call or e-mail committee members before activities to remind them that Tot Shabbat is coming up and let them know what kind of help is needed. A typical message might be, "Tot Shabbat is coming up this Saturday. We have a great activity planned and need your help. Please plan on arriving early to help set up or sticking around afterward to help clean up. Be sure to remind the other families in your child's class to join us. Thank you for your help making Tot Shabbat great." The chair stands up at Tot Shabbat events and introduces him- or herself and the committee, so everyone knows who they can talk to if they want to know more or if they want to help out. The chair should be talking to the families in attendance and personally welcoming any new families.

Committee members participate in the planning meeting and can take on other roles, such as providing challah and juice, picking up or ordering supplies, setting up and cleaning up, or doing publicity for and outreach at events. Most of this committee work is done at the events themselves, contributing to the sense that "as long as you are already going to be there, become part of the committee."

The most important role of Tot Shabbat committee members is building a social network. Committee members do their best advertising when it is word of mouth; parents talking in the parking lot about attending Tot Shabbat creates a social atmosphere. Parents who feel invested in the program will talk about it to other parents; they will invite other families to attend as if it were their event. Tot Shabbat committee members should be encouraged to invite other families and to welcome new families to Tot Shabbat; the social connection of being welcomed by another family goes a long way toward persuading these families to return in the future. One of the most visible measures of program success is the number of families present. When Tot Shabbat committee members feel personally responsible for the success of the program, they will make an effort to encourage more families to attend and to ensure that anyone already at Tot Shabbat will want to come back again.

The ways to leverage the committee are limited only by the imagination of the chairperson and the interests of the members, so tap into the skills of the committee members. When I was chair of the Tot Shabbat committee at Ahavat Shalom, my husband, who is a graphic designer, made all the flyers advertising Tot Shabbat. If you have a member who is a scrapbook fan, you could start a Tot Shabbat scrapbook; a photographer could ensure that photos of Tot Shabbat make it onto the temple Web site; a social planner could expand Tot Shabbat into a potluck picnic after the official Tot Shabbat activity.

If you are a Synaplex synagogue, you should encourage a member of the Tot Shabbat committee to serve on the Synaplex committee to ensure cooperation between Tot Shabbat and Synaplex. Often Tot Shabbat fits quite seamlessly as a self-contained unit into a larger Synaplex program; maximizing this connection is a great way to lead early childhood families into everything else the synagogue has to offer. Visit www.synaplex.org for more information.

At some point at every Tot Shabbat program, the leader should publicly thank—by name—the members of the Tot Shabbat committee. They should also be mentioned in newsletters and other public forums, not only so new families will know who they can talk to with questions or to volunteer, but so that the members of the committee will know that their work is noticed and appreciated.

Year-to-Year Transitions

To ease transition from year to year, I suggest creating a binder or folder that contains all the information about Tot Shabbat: what projects were done (so you don't repeat too frequently), notes from the committee chair on what programs worked the best and which should not be repeated, sources of supplies, and any flyers or other advertising that were produced. If you have members with children who will only be of Tot Shabbat age for another year or two, enlist their help in recruiting new members and smoothing the transition.

Conclusion

Although I have suggested that Tot Shabbat can be one of the easiest committees to serve on, I also believe that it is one of the most important. While any committee involvement increases a feeling of ownership and connection to the school or program, serving on the Tot Shabbat committee creates a feeling of ownership about Shabbat and about worship services. Parents who may start off intimidated by Shabbat or by services develop a connection that can lead them to participate in family services and then "regular" services as their children grow up. Parents can develop a sense of involvement in shaping the synagogue experience and a sense of responsibility for making Shabbat worship meaningful for all ages. A Tot Shabbat committee gives parents a sense of investment in the program that fuels a desire to see it succeed.

Part IV

What Do
Stories Add
to Tot Shabbat?

10

Choosing a Wonderful Story

Diane Person

Reading, whether being read to or reading on one's own, is absolutely a thinking process; it is an interactive process between the author/reader and the audience/ listener/reader. Children bring all their life experiences to story events, from knowing how to be good listeners to knowing how to translate what they're hearing into meaningful information and ideas. They should be able to come away from a shared story time with new insights about how other people live or have lived and thoughts about how to incorporate these ideas into their own lives and behaviors in ways that are consistent with Jewish and community beliefs. With their limited life experiences, children use stories as a way to look out into the bigger world around them and beyond their neighborhoods, to try on different roles and behaviors, and to examine how they might respond to different situations that confront them. They use stories to try on different roles and prepare for new situations they will soon encounter in school, on the playground, and within the family. Young children are just starting to reach out beyond their immediate families and make friends. Award-winning children's books, such as Caldecott Award titles, feature subtle themes, usually unstated, that allow young children to explore valid responses that have applications in their own lives. They see how storybook characters respond to difficult situations and overcome adversity.

We see young children wearing capes, masks, or ferocious warrior costumes or dressed in pink with fairy wings hoping to be chosen by some untested prince. They are trying on different behavior models of popular cartoon characters that never have to overcome doubts and fears, change, and grow up; they only get to "live happily ever after." These models are inconsistent with Jewish ethics and morality, the very things we are trying to instill in our children. And yet such Jewish stories are readily available from both mainstream trade and small sectarian publishers. Stop and think of familiar characters from the Bible; all of them relate tales that start in childhood and follow these traditional heroes into adulthood. We all know the story of Noah and the ark, David and Goliath, and Joseph and his brothers. We celebrate the story of Joseph from his youth tending his father's flock with his brothers and going on to become a forgiving, loving brother. Does any story compare with that of Moses, heart-wrenchingly surrendered by his mother to save his life and starting that life floating in a basket among the reeds? What princess story compares with that of Esther, who gets to marry the king and then saves the Jewish people? It is little wonder that dressing as Esther is the most popular costume among little girls at Purim. Who would not like to start as an orphan and then become the woman who saves her people? Can Wonder Woman or Cinderella really compete with Queen Esther?

With the advent of mandatory public elementary education, widespread literacy, and modern technology in the publishing industry, a new market was created: publishing books intended solely for the pleasure of children. These books were meant to delight and amuse young readers, but without a ready cadre of authors, publishers turned to stories that were easily accessible and free of charge; with the addition of illustrations, the familiar became new again. In fact, the first picture book to win a Caldecott Award, in 1938, was Helen Dean Fish's *Animals of the Bible*, illustrated by D. P. Lathrop. As children's publishing has become more attuned to the developmental and emotional needs of children, so, too, has the variety and quality of Bible-based children's books expanded and kept pace with the emotional development of children as we understand it today. While these picture books are based, for the most part, on the lives of well-known biblical characters, thematically they are significant in terms of issues that confront contemporary children today. These issues include sibling rivalry, saving the environment, resolution of human conflict, and responding to peer pressure, all of them central to living an ethical Jewish life in the midst of a secular world.

The stories that have inspired adults and children for generations speak directly to the worries, both spoken and unspoken, and the ambitions of young children. Little boys in their capes and hoods with their plastic swords and wooden sticks in hand play at being superheroes who arrive on scene with their magical powers in hand, ready to do battle and save the world. They have nothing to learn, nothing to practice; they have simply arrived full-blown on the landscape. They and other TV cartoon characters never have to make decisions about being obedient to authority figures or wrestle with questions of morality, of what's right or wrong, good or evil. Their triumphs are hollow. No adult figure has been there to guide them. In Bible stories there is an adult figure that guides, protects, and intervenes, and ultimately it is God. Which of these scenarios is a more desirable example of a role model for a young child, something against which he can measure himself? Let's look at the biblical story of David as it is told in dozens of versions for young children.

In the story of David as portrayed in Leonard Everett Fisher's *David and Goliath* (Holiday House, 1993), Emily Little's *David and the Giant* (Random House, 1987), and Barbara Cohen's *David: A Biography* (Clarion, 1995), among others, we see a transformation from naïve boyhood and innocent bravado to mature adult able to command the respect of his people, a leader guided by the moral decisions he makes. As adults we know David did not always make the right decisions, that he was a man, not a plastic cartoon figure who never had to make choices, consider consequences, or base decisions on the ethics of the situation. Unlike cartoon figures, David and other Bible heroes have to live with the results of the choices they make. As the youngest son—a not insignificant fact—David is overprotected by his father and frequently teased by his older brothers, who are sent to fight Goliath. In these dramatic retellings there are scenes of sibling rivalry, a well-known emotion among children, but David's hardy resolve and success guide him in his task, and he wins the accolades of his stunned brothers. David is a champion and is helped to maintain his faith in God through God's appointed delegate, Samuel. The idea of a benevolent parent or other close relative—God in this case—who watches over a child is reassuring to children. The figure of Goliath is a favorite in children's stories; think of Jack and the Beanstalk, Peter Pan, and St. George and the Dragon. But in David children have an opportunity, through hearing the story, to try on the role of the favored, protected younger sibling struggling to prove he can be as brave and strong as his big brothers and stop their constant teasing and bullying. The story of David, of proving that the smallest is not necessarily the least significant and that hurtful words are not OK to use against one's siblings, is too important to not be taught in the Tot Shabbat setting.

In stories about Noah and the ark, Adam and Eve, and Jonah and the whale, children see that there are consequences to bad behavior, but a benevolent parent/God can give you another chance. These three stories are the most frequently retold in picture book format and are among children's favorites. The stories themselves are as exciting and as implausible as Transformers or Power Rangers. Just imagine Stan Lee or Hanna-Barbera creating a story about a man who disobeys orders, refuses to do as he is told, runs away in the opposite direction, and then, as punishment, gets swallowed by a very large fish. What saves the story of Jonah in picture books such as Mordicai Gerstein's *Jonah and the Two Great Fish* (Simon and Schuster, 1997), Miriam Chaikin's "Jonah and the Whale" in *Children's Bible Stories from Genesis to Daniel* (Dial, 1993), and Lorenz Graham's *How God Fix Jonah* (Boyds Mills Press, 2000) from becoming a situation comedy cartoon is Jonah's eventual awareness that only he has the internal strength to save himself and complete his appointed task. This is the heart of the story, not the action-packed adventure that children love to hear about. It is about Jonah refusing to do what he has been told to do, running away as children dream of doing, and only reluctantly obeying God's command. It is about being afraid and behaving grudgingly, halfheartedly, before he is certain that he is doing the right thing and can be successful at his assigned task. It is a monumental realization that it is up to him to make the independent choice of whether to accept the task God has set before him. Helping children learn to make good choices, to know what is right and acceptable in the eyes of God, community, and family, is a big step in learning to live Jewishly as adults. There is, perhaps, no greater lesson we can help the children in our care to learn. The world today is a very difficult place, and navigating one's way in it may seem like an impossibly frightening task for young children, but with examples of heroes from the Bible firmly before their eyes, children are able to develop self-confidence in their decision-making powers. The story of Jonah also shows children how God, like their parents, offers a second chance when he forgives the people of Nineveh and does not destroy them along with their city. Parallels to the story of Jonah also appear in contemporary picture books. Maurice Sendak's *Where the Wild Things Are* (Harper & Row, 1963) reiterates the same theme of forgiveness; when Max defiantly refuses to obey his mother's command to behave, he gets sent to his room, just as Jonah is sent to the belly of the whale. Both flee across the sea; Jonah flees to Tarshish, and Max flees to "where the wild things are," but both soon learn to accept the reasonable authority of a caring adult. And, like Jonah, when Max sees the error of his ways, he is forgiven by a compassionate mother who has kept his dinner hot and waiting for him, just as a compassionate God forgives Jonah and the people of Nineveh.

In its most recent retellings, the story of Noah and the ark has been transformed into a cautionary save-the-environment, save-the-earth story. The rock performer Sting first wrote the music and lyrics for a song called "Rock Steady" in 1987; in 2001 he published a picture book version using the song illustrated with crayon-bright drawings of a universe without political divisions. Riding a camel taxi across the city, a man and a woman arrive at the ark, volunteering to help feed and care for the animals; the importance of volunteering and caring for our neighbors is unmistakable. The couple is soon busy helping to wash and care for the animals but concerned about whether the ark is steady as a rock, whether the earth is a firm rock on which to build a firm foundation of life. As the story progresses, it is clear that Noah is a man who obeys God and is following the commandment of God as he has heard it on the radio. The theme in *Rock Steady* is that living by God's commandment to protect and preserve the environment keeps people firmly rooted on earth and that the earth will provide for all people as long as people cooperate and take care of the earth.

Each chapter in *The Flood Tales* by Richard Monte (Pavilion, 2000) retells an aspect of the familiar Noah story emphasizing a contemporary aspect of moral concern to Jewish people everywhere. Each chapter presents ideas about living an ethical life as the Jewish community understands those beliefs today. There are chapters that explore our treatment of the environment, our relationship with animals, ecological concerns about extinction and our responsibility to help avoid such a fate for all the different species, and a chapter on gender issues and treating people as equals. The story "The Vegetarian Supper" is especially appropriate for young children. In this chapter the concept of caring for the environment is told in biblical terms, with the flood as a direct result of people not caring for the environment but rather allowing it to become polluted. Noah muses about whether the dumping of toxic waste material into rivers and seeping into the soil has caused the extinction of several species and the nutrients in soil that allow food to grow. He wonders whether the flood is retribution for man's careless treatment of the earth that God has entrusted to humans or whether it is a bountiful God's gift of renewal to his people, just as a parent gives a second chance to a repentant child.

For the very youngest children who still appreciate a nearly wordless picture book, Ann Jonas's *Aardvarks, Disembark!* (Greenwillow, 1990) tells the flood story as a cautionary tale about extinction and caring for the remaining species. Interestingly, the book is held vertically, with the ark resting on top of Mount Ararat and a dramatic rainbow framing the sky around it as the pairs of animals descend. Noah assembles the pairs of animals and orders them, in alphabetical order, to leave the ark. The animals are shown dispersing to the four corners of the earth as Noah admonishes them, "Take good care of yourselves. Take good care, everyone." The thematic concept that life endures is emphasized with the reassuring words "Life began again." There is much to discuss with young children: how Noah worked to protect and ensure the survival of so many species just as "we" can do today to help save endangered species; what God's role was in the story of Noah and the ark; and the meanings of the rainbow and the doves.

Another hugely popular theme in children's literature is the beautiful princess who seems to have everything as a young girl but then has to grow up quickly when she is faced with making a choice—the choice between the easy fairy-tale decision or the ethical, moral real-life choice. The story of Esther is the story of the journey from childhood to maturity, of becoming a member of the Jewish community, of considering the survival of the Jewish people, of moving from self-centeredness to altruism. In most picture books about Esther, her two outstanding characteristics are her beauty and her obedience. These attributes permeate picture-book retellings of Esther's story and emphasize how these two characteristics are used to save the Jewish community, not for Esther's personal gain. One instance of her obedience working with her newfound courage occurs in Rita Golden Gelman's *Queen Esther Saves Her People* (Scholastic, 1998). When she goes to meet King Ahasuerus, she holds her head high and meets his gaze eye to eye, a courageous choice that goes against Mordecai's advice to be demure and obedient. Her beauty serves her well in Mordicai Gerstein's *Queen Esther the Morning Star* (Simon and Schuster, 2000). When she prepares to meet the king, she is dressed simply. It is Esther's purity and ability to use her beauty to help save the Jewish nation that distinguish this story from traditional fairy tales, where beauty is its own reward, the tool used to win the handsome prince's hand.

In Tomie dePaola's picture book *Queen Esther* (Harper & Row, 1986), Esther has her uncle Mordecai as a role model to follow. First, readers see and hear Mordecai refusing to submit to Haman's order to the populace to bow down to him because Jews obey Jewish law and "bow only to God," not to people. For young children listening to this story, the interpretation is that obedience has to be just and reasonable, that individuals have the obligation to determine which orders to obey and which are unjust and should be disobeyed. This is a powerful lesson for children to learn, not only in terms of practicing their religion but as a critical lesson as they get older and don't always have adult supervision. Being obedient and making good choices are both religious Jewish imperatives and moral imperatives as children grow to adolescence.

Major trade publishers are very careful to make sure that their picture books are appropriate for the youngest listeners and readers. They are sensitive to thematic appropriateness and inclusiveness of different racial, religious, ethnic, and gender groups and people with disabilities. While any picture book with an obvious biblical setting would seem appropriate for a Tot Shabbat, this is not always so. Some books may, however unintentionally, present one group of people in a stereotypical way or in a version that is inconsistent with accepted Jewish values and practices. Sometimes a picture book will distort accepted Jewish beliefs and versions of Bible stories. At the same time, books with a contemporary realistic setting will underscore themes that are integral to Jewish beliefs and values. Many picture books for this age group emphasize how to be a friend, how to include children with disabilities, and how to be a cooperative sibling and depict loving family relationships, often intergenerational. By emphasizing the relevant developmental themes discussed above, picture books and stories are appropriate to the concerns of young children and a great tool for teaching during Tot Shabbat.

How to Read Stories in a Group Setting

Picture books are very effective sources for storytelling and reading aloud with children of all ages in a group setting. They provide a compelling place for listeners to focus their attention and be drawn into the storytelling event as if they were characters within the story. They are drawn into the events of the story and become participants in the action, able to assume any character they choose that is represented in the illustrations. Before the page is turned they are able to imagine what their favorite character will do next. At this point the reading or storytelling event is no longer a passive event but very much an active, participatory event that will resound long after the story is read.

Reading aloud is a wonderful way to share ideas with children, ideas living within the context of Jewish morality. There are several things a reader must do before sitting down to read in front of a group of preschool-age children. The success of the event is in the preparation, just as a musician practices before a concert, a chef spends hours chopping ingredients before assembling a four-star dinner, or an athlete trains before the competition starts.

Once a book has been selected according to the thematic guidelines discussed in the preceding section, you are ready to confirm that your selection is appropriate to the developmental age of the children in the Tot Shabbat age group. Each book should arouse children's imaginations, leading them to think of how they would feel and respond in different situations compared with characters in the story and with aspects of Jewish living discussed earlier in the class session.

Reading and storytelling are best done in an informal, comfortable setting where the reader is in as close personal contact as possible with the children. The children may be seated in an informal semicircle around the storyteller, creating an intimate atmosphere that draws the children into the story experience. This creates a familiarity with the storyteller that makes it feel more like you are telling the story directly to each child just as you would in a one-on-one storytelling event. When the children are able to sit close to you and see the details of the illustrations, they see fine artwork, the equal of what they can see in museums. Hold the book with your arm extended so they can clearly see the illustrations and connect the words of the story with its corresponding illustration. Tot Shabbat participants will soon be in a formal school setting where they will learn to read. Exposing them to the concepts of how a book is organized—left to right, top to bottom—without overtly teaching helps prepare them for a formal school program. But most important, young children become aware that following along, paying careful attention to the illustrations, allows them to "read" the story right along with the teacher. As famed illustrator and graphic designer Milton Glaser writes in *Drawing Is Thinking* (Overlook Press, 2008), "Illustrations are a way to look at the world"; they are "a way to understand and experience the world." A successful picture book invites pre-readers to follow along with the storyteller and "read" the story on their own. The illustrations provide more story detail than the brief text, often allowing for a subtext to be told in pictures, as *in Joseph Had a Little Overcoat* by Simms Taback (Viking, 1999).

First read the story to yourself, making sure the story and language are appropriate for the intended age group. Further, make certain that the story you are about to read is one that you like. Your enthusiasm, or lack of it, will be obvious to the children through your voice, facial expressions, and body language. Choose a book that can be read completely at one Tot Shabbat. Children will lose the thread of the story if they have to wait until the following week to hear the conclusion. Practice reading the story out loud several times until you have it almost memorized and can read it without having to keep your eyes on the page. Read it a few times in front of a mirror so you can monitor your facial expressions. Practice until you can read it without stumbling over unfamiliar names while lifting your face from the page to make eye contact with your listeners. Your voice should not become a droning monotone; instead, follow the phrasing of the book as suggested by the punctuation and action, raising your voice in the action sentences, reading more slowly and quietly when the characters are deliberating a solution and at the conclusion. At other times use your own natural speaking voice. In this way you convey the mood, plot, and theme of the book.

When you start, after the children are seated, hold up the book for children to see while reading the author's name and title. Ask them to predict what they think the story will be about; this creates interest and helps them to settle down and listen. Afterwards, come back to their predictions and discuss in what ways their predictions were right and where they diverged. It is always helpful to have some kind of an object or device that will motivate their interest and help young children to concentrate; a small basket, a small boat, a tiara, a large rock will raise interest that relates directly to the story about to be read.

Afterwards, ask children to share their favorite part of the story, to explain why one character was their favorite, and to talk about why their favorite story character behaved a certain way, how she could have behaved differently, how else the story could have ended, and whether the story reminds them of anything they talked/learned about that day. Ask how this story relates to their own lives or experiences in any way. It is important not to ask questions that simply elicit "yes" or "no" answers. Following these simple guidelines is sure to make storytelling a happy experience and an important part of your Tot Shabbat.

Bibliography

Chaikin, Miriam. *Children's Bible Stories from Genesis to Daniel.* New York: Dial Books for Young Readers, 1993.

Cohen, Barbara. *David: A Biography.* New York: Clarion, 1995.

DePaola, Tomie. *Queen Esther: A Bible Story Book.* New York: Harper & Row, 1986.

Fish, Helen Dean, adapter. *Animals of the Bible: A Picture Book.* Illustrated by Dorothy P. Lathrop. New York: Frederick A. Stokes, 1937.

Fisher, Leonard Everett. *David and Goliath.* New York: Holiday House, 1993.

Gelman, Rita Golden. *Queen Esther Saves Her People.* Illustrated by Frané Lessac. New York: Scholastic, 1998.

Gerstein, Mordicai. *Jonah and the Two Great Fish.* New York: Simon and Schuster, 1997.

———. *Queen Esther the Morning Star.* New York: Simon and Schuster, 2000.

Glaser, Milton. *Drawing Is Thinking.* New York: Overlook Press, 2008.

Graham, Lorenz. *How God Fix Jonah.* 1st rev. ed. Illustrated by Ashley Bryan. Honesdale, Pa.: Boyds Mills Press, 2000.

Jonas, Ann. *Aardvarks, Disembark!* New York: Greenwillow, 1990.

Little, Emily. *David and the Giant.* Illustrated by Hans Wilhelm. New York: Random House, 1987.

Monte, Richard. *The Flood Tales.* Illustrated by Izhar Cohen. London: Pavilion Books, 2000.

Sendak, Maurice. *Where the Wild Things Are.* New York: Harper & Row, 1963.

Sting. *Rock Steady: A Story of Noah's Ark.* Illustrated by Hugh Whyte. New York: HarperCollins, 2001.

Taback, Simms. *Joseph Had a Little Overcoat.* New York: Viking, 1999.

11

Interactive
Storytelling Techniques

Eva Grayzel

No one loves a story more than a young child—except maybe his or her parents! Children and adults of all ages love stories. Telling stories in an effective way does not need to be difficult. Here are some ideas for how to use stories during Tot Shabbat, bedtime, holiday dinners, or anytime.

If you are telling a story from a book, do not feel tied to the text. Some wonderful books have too much text, or text written on too high a level for the Tot Shabbat age group. Feel free to **tell** the story. Use the book as a guideline for yourself. A good way to prepare is to read a few sentences of the book and then put it in your own words. It might feel a bit risky at first, but this is a very effective technique. One way to capture and exaggerate the drama as you tell the story is by using action words: laughs, stamps feet, shakes, cries, screams, points, grimaces. Feel free to add details. One way to do this is to give the character an action, for example:

- If your story has "a beautiful woman," have her stroke her hair and sway her hips.
- If your story has "a sad man," have him frown, drag his feet, and hang his head.
- If the story says, "She was confused," have her pace the room and rub her chin.
- If the story says, "He was shocked," have him jump out of his chair and throw his arms up.

If you can't think of what to say when you read or tell the story, ask the children, "He was angry. What did he do?" They can then tell you what a person might do when he is angry, and you can add their answers to the story: "Yes, he stamped his foot, he raised his voice, he put his hands on his hips and cried." Feel free to act out these actions as you read or tell the story.

As you describe a character and his or her actions, you may ask a child to act them out. If the children acting out the story are old enough, you can give the character something to say too. Then your story will come to life! If the character repeats the same word or phrase throughout the story, teach a child or all the children to say the phrase. An example might be if the character is told over and over to go somewhere and he repeatedly says, "I won't go!" Cue the child/children to say the character's line whenever it comes up. Or come up with a little ditty to repeat during the story. For example, whenever the character thinks about what to do (it's always good to think before you act!), "He rubs his chin, scratches his head, taps the floor, and thinks some more." Once the children know this little ditty and/or the hand motions that can go with it, they can repeat it during the story. If you have trouble thinking of a little ditty, take a nursery rhyme or a song with a simple tune that everyone knows and change the words. When you include the children in this way, it really makes the children part of the story. If you would like to take this technique one step further (depending on the developmental level of the children and the time that you have), you can have the children and their parents create the little ditty, rhyme, or song themselves. There is nothing better than giving children the opportunity to use their imaginations.

As you can see, when using a storybook, it is fun to be creative and not feel tied to the text. It is also possible to be creative with the illustrations. Many books have beautiful illustrations, but for something different, give the children paper to draw on and have them draw the scenes from the story themselves, rather than showing them the illustrations. Here again, the children can bring their imaginations to the story.

It is also very important to emphasize the values you want to teach. You do not need to tell the children how to behave; let them experience it through the story. One way to do this is to choose children to play particular parts. As you tell the story and the children act it out, talk about how the characters are feeling when they are treated a certain way. This way the children can safely explore feelings and behaviors through the characters in the story. This technique will teach children empathy and boost their self-esteem.

Another way to enrich a story is to add Hebrew words or *b'rachot* that the children recently learned into the story. Use a Hebrew vocabulary word in place of an English word, or adapt the story to have elements of the holiday you are teaching. It requires a bit of creativity, but it also enriches the story and reinforces the material being taught.

If you have the time, some ways to further expand a story are to gather simple costumes and props to use: hats, vests, robes, scarves, costume jewelry, and so on.

When I prepare to tell a story I do the following:

1. Outline the story by scenes (five to seven scenes).
2. List the characters.
3. Choose the values/facts to emphasize.
4. Think about the best room arrangement.
5. Gather any costumes or props.

Here is what my index cards say for the Jonah story:

1. Five scenes:
    A. Jonah is lazy, asked to go to city of Nineveh, Jonah runs away to boat.
    B. Jonah gets on boat, conversation with captain, everyone rows and he goes to sleep, storm begins.
    C. Sailor wakes Jonah, Jonah realizes the storm is because of him, tells captain to throw him overboard . . . they do.
    D. Jonah ends up in whale, asks for forgiveness, is spit up on shore and goes to Nineveh.
    E. People of Nineveh are stealing, fighting . . . Jonah tells them what could be, they agree to change.
2. Character list: Jonah, God, captain, sailor(s), chair for whale
3. Values/facts to emphasize: how to say "I'm sorry," accepting apologies
4. Audience group part: the sailors, waves of stormy ocean, "bad" people of Nineveh.
5. Repeating refrains: "Jonah, Jonah, Jonah and the Whale"

All these different ideas and techniques are effective because they address many different learning styles and involve the children themselves in the story. These approaches to storytelling encourage the children to experience the story, not just as listeners but as participants. It may seem a bit daunting at first, but it is fun, and as you get better at it you can do a lot of teaching, in fact **all** of it, within the context of a story.

12

Jewish Story Bibliography*

Rachel Kamin

While a traditional Shabbat service might include a sermon or a *d'var Torah*, sharing an age-appropriate story can be a wonderful addition to a Tot Shabbat service. Stories can be read, retold, acted out, or sung. The story can relate to an upcoming holiday, connect with the weekly *parashah*, or just be a good Jewish book. When looking for a gem to share during Tot Shabbat, look for books and stories with the following characteristics:

- **Know the story, love the story:** Start with stories that you know and love. Don't expect to pick up a book a couple minutes before Tot Shabbat begins and read it for the first time in front of your audience. Even if it is a wonderful story and you are a fabulous narrator, chances are your reading will not be very engaging, interactive, or successful. Read and rehearse the story several times in advance so that you are thoroughly familiar with it. Plan for opportunities to interact with the audience, substitute or define unfamiliar terms, shorten or paraphrase if needed, and prepare props, costumes, or visual aids. Also, only share stories that you are passionate and enthusiastic about, and have fun—the more fun you are having, the more fun your audience will have!
- **KISS = Keep It Short and Simple:** Choose stories that are short and simple and that can involve the entire audience. Keep in mind that the younger and larger the group, the simpler, bigger, and bolder the characters and props have to be. Don't be afraid to shorten and simplify stories to make them more accessible to your audience. However, if in doing so you lose the magic, cohesiveness, and fluidity of the story, skip it and find something that is more age appropriate.
- **Patterns and rituals:** Look for stories with patterns in the plot, recurring phrases, and opportunities to add hand motions and sound effects. And,

---

*Based on "Storytelling Bag of Tricks," a handout created by Cheryl Levy, a children's librarian, teacher, educator, and storyteller from Midland, Michigan.

don't be afraid to add more repetition to your retelling. For example, in *The Tale of Meshka the Kvetch* by Carol Chapman, Meshka begins some of her complaints with "Oy Vey," but it is more fun to have the audience groan, "Oy Vey," every time Meshka complains. *The Matzah That Papa Brought Home* by Fran Manushkin is a natural choice for adding hand motions and sound effects.

- **Personalize:** Select stories that can be personalized for your audience, your congregation, or your community. If the story features a rabbi, give the character the name of your congregation's rabbi. Change the setting to your hometown, add other "insider" details, or even retell a story in the first person as if you are the protagonist and the story happened to you.

- **Add music:** Stories with lines or refrains that can be sung or can be connected to a song increase participation and add another layer of interaction. For example, teach your audience the song "There's a Dinosaur" (available on *I've Got a Shabbat Feeling* by Andi Joseph and *From Shabbat to Havdalah: A Preschool Musical Adventure* by the Minneapolis Sabes JCC) when you read *Dinosaur on Shabbat* by Diane Levin Rauchwerger. Sing the familiar frog song when you read *The Littlest Frog* by Sylvia Rouss. *How the Rosh Hashanah Challah Became Round* by Sylvia Epstein and *Once Upon a Shabbos* by Jacqueline Jules include refrains that easily can be sung to any tune of your choice. And books like *Five Little Gefiltes* by Dave Horowitz and *I Have a Little Driedel* by Maxie Baum can naturally be sung in their entirety.

- **Keep records:** Keep notes on how and when you tell a story and how you can do it better next time. The nice thing about Tot Shabbat is that the audience changes every couple of years, so you can always repeat a story. By keeping track of the stories you tell on note cards, a spreadsheet, or another method, you will develop a list of "tried and true" stories that you can always refer back to.

- **Consult resources:** Still can't find the perfect story? Turn to *Jewish Values Finder: A Guide to Values in Jewish Children's Literature* by Linda R. Silver, or go to www.ajljewishvalues.org for a listing of nearly one thousand carefully selected children's books that promote Jewish values. Each entry includes an annotation, age-level recommendations, subject headings, and relevant Jewish values. From the Web site, you can search the database by title, author, subject, or value and narrow your search by age level. Another invaluable resource, especially if you looking for a story on a specific theme or subject or you remember hearing a wonderful story but don't know where to find it, is *Jewish Story Finder: A Guide to 363 Tales Listing Subjects and Sources* by Sharon Barcan Elswit. Hundreds of stories are indexed by title and subject, and each entry includes a summary, subjects, and a listing of different versions of the story with their sources. And, of course, you can always ask librarians, teachers, rabbis, educators, storytellers, and other book lovers for suggestions and recommendations—most people are more than happy to share their ideas and experiences.

Keep in mind that many wonderful stories and picture books will need to be retold, instead of read straight through, to make them more accessible, engaging, and interactive. Adapt, edit, and improvise until you find your most comfortable method of presenting a story. Don't force yourself to follow the text word for word or include every character—you will always need to adjust to your audience. To help you get started, below is a list of recommended books and resources to use during a Tot Shabbat program. The list is divided into three parts: picture books that can be read aloud, books that need to be retold, and collections of stories to retell. Borrow these books from your synagogue library or your local public library, or purchase them from a local or online bookseller. Remember that your local public library can borrow almost any book for you via interlibrary loan. But be sure to plan ahead and request titles in advance. Also, while some may be out of print, many of these recommendations are available used from online booksellers at very reasonable prices. This list is by no means comprehensive but represents the best of what's available for young children and their families. It will hopefully get you started on your quest to find the perfect Jewish story to share at Tot Shabbat!

Recommended Books to Read Aloud during Tot Shabbat

The following picture books can be read with little or no editing or adapting.

Abraham, Michelle Shapiro. *Shabbat Shalom!* Illustrated by Ann Kofsky. New York: URJ Press, 2003. ISBN: 0807408662.

Simple prose explains the rituals of Shabbat with a repetitive refrain—"We bring Shabbat into our home by giving *tzedakah* [or "blessing candles," "blessing children," "blessing wine," "blessing bread," "thanking God"], Shabbat Shalom!"—which can make this a very participatory reading. The blessings are also included in Hebrew, transliteration, and English translation. A musical companion is also available on CD: *Shabbat Shalom! Jewish Children's Songs for Shabbat.*

Baum, Maxie. *I Have a Little Dreidel.* Illustrated by Julie Paschkis. New York: Scholastic, 2006. ISBN: 0439649978.

This version of the familiar song cleverly adds new verses detailing a contemporary family's celebration of Chanukah. Besides just playing dreidel, the family makes latkes, lights the menorah, and enjoys a delicious dinner together. Since the book is oversized and the illustrations are bold and vibrant, show the pictures as you sing the book.

Chapman, Carol. *The Tale of Meshka the Kvetch.* Illustrated by Arnold Lobel. New York: Dutton, 1980. ISBN: 0525407456.

When everything Meshka complains about comes true, she must finally learn to stop kvetching and be happy with what she has. Have the audience participate by shouting "*Oy vey*" in their "kvetchiest" voices every time Meshka begins to complain.

Davis, Aubrey. *Bagels from Benny.* **Illustrated by Dušan Petričić. Toronto: Kids Can Press, 2003. ISBN: 1553374177.**

Benny decides that the best way to thank God for the delicious bagels that his grandfather bakes is to leave them in the ark on Friday afternoon for God to enjoy. A touching twist on a traditional folktale with a beautiful message about how a small act of kindness can help make the world a better place. Musical tie-in: "Bagels and Cream Cheese" by Joel Frankel on the *Ship of Chocolate Chips* CD.

Epstein, Sylvia B. *How the Rosh Hashanah Challah Became Round.* **Illustrated by Hagit Migron. Jerusalem: Gefen Publishing House, 1993. ISBN: 9652290955.**

A fun explanation for why we eat a round challah on Rosh HaShanah. After boasting to his siblings about being the only one old enough to help in Papa's bakery, Yossi accidentally falls down the stairs, and all the perfectly shaped challot became fat and round instead.

Getzel. *The Stonecutter Who Wanted to Be Rich.* **New York: C.I.S. Publishers, 1990. ISBN: 156062030.**

A simple story based on the verse from *Pirkei Avot:* "Who is rich? One who is satisfied with what he has." Create large posters of a king, the sun, a cloud, the wind, and a mountain to help illustrate the story.

Gilman, Phoebe. *Something from Nothing.* **New York: Scholastic, 1992. ISBN: 059073802X.**

In this version of the favorite Jewish folktale, Joseph's worn-out baby blanket becomes a jacket, a vest, a tie, a hankerchief, and a button. Other versions of the story include *Joseph Had a Little Overcoat* by Simms Taback and *Bit by Bit* by Steve Sanfield. The song "I Had an Old Coat" is available on *The Elephant Party* CD by Sharon, Lois & Bram.

Goldin, Barbara Diamond. *A Mountain of Blintzes.* **Illustrated by Anik McGrory. San Diego: Harcourt, 2001. ISBN: 0152019022.**

A group of loving, resourceful siblings find a way to gather the ingredients needed for their festive Shavuot meal, despite Mama and Papa's failed attempt to put money aside for the holiday.

Hirsh, Marilyn. *The Rabbi and the Twenty-Nine Witches.* **New York: Holiday House, 1976. ISBN: 0823402703.**

Twenty-nine mean and ugly witches prevent an entire village from enjoying the light of a full moon until the rabbi finally comes up with a plan to outsmart them.

Horowitz, Dave. *Five Little Gefiltes.* **New York: G.P. Putnam's Sons, 2007. ISBN: 9780399246081.**

"Five little gefiltes went out one day, out of the jar and far away. Mama Gefilte cried out OY VEY! But only four little gefiltes came back that day." This hilarious twist on the classic "Five Little Ducks" song will have kids and adults laughing hysterically. Create gefilte fish stick puppets for an even livelier sing-along.

Howland, Naomi. *Matzah Man.* **New York: Clarion/Houghton Mifflin, 2002. ISBN: 061811750.**

"Hot from the oven I jumped and ran, so clever and quick, I'm the Matzah Man!" is the refrain in this Passover version of "The Gingerbread Boy." *The Runaway Latkes* by Leslie Kimmelman is another cute Jewish "Gingerbread" story.

Jules, Jacqueline. *Once Upon a Shabbos.* **Illustrated by Katherine Janus Kahn. Rockville, MD: Kar-Ben Copies, 1998. ISBN: 1580130216.**

When a bear keeps stealing the honey needed for the Shabbat kugel, Bubbe must take things into her own hands—she invites the bear to come for dinner! Musical tie-in: "We're Going on a Bear Hunt" from the book and CD by Michael Rosen or from the *Let's Go!* CD by Susie Tallman & Friends.

Kimmel, Eric A. *Zigazak! A Magical Hanukkah Night.* **Illustrated by Jon Goodell. New York: Doubleday Book for Young Readers, 2001. ISBN: 0385326521.**

From the most prolific Chanukah storyteller comes this story of two evil spirits who attempt to ruin one town's Chanukah celebration. See also: *The Chanukah Guest, Hershel and the Hanukkah Goblins, The Magic Dreidels, When Mindy Saved Hanukkah,* and *The Jar of Fools: Eight Hanukkah Stories from Chelm.*

Manushkin, Fran. *The Matzah That Papa Brought Home.* **Illustrated by Ned Bittinger. New York: Scholastic Inc, 1995. ISBN: 0590471465.**

With cumulative rhymes, Papa brings home the matzah, Mama prepares a feast, the family joins together for the seder, and all of the rituals are performed before everyone turns in for the night. Have participants act out each rhyme, with a sound effect or movement.

Renberg, Dalia Hardof. *King Solomon and the Bee.* **Illustrated by Ruth Heller. New York: HarperCollins Publishers, 1994. ISBN: 0060558997.**

When a small bee accidentally stings King Solomon on the nose, the bee finds a resourceful way to prove his worth by helping the king outsmart the Queen of Sheba.

Rauchwerger, Diane. *Dinosaur on Shabbat.* **Illustrated by Jason Wolff. Minneapolis: Kar-Ben Publishing, 2006. ISBN: 9781580131599.**

A friendly, oversized dinosaur arrives to celebrate Shabbat with a young boy and his family. In silly, rhyming text, Dino tries to help with Shabbat preparations: setting the table, lighting the candles, pouring the wine, and blessing the challah. He also joins the family in the synagogue on Shabbat morning and participates in *Havdalah.* Pair with "The Dinosaur Song" available on *I've Got a Shabbat Feeling* by Andi Joseph and *From Shabbat to Havdalah: A Preschool Musical Adventure* by the Minneapolis Sabes JCC. See also: *Dinosaur on Passover* and *Dinosaur on Hanukkah.*

Rouss, Sylvia. *The Littlest Frog.* **Illustrated by Holly Hannon. New York: Pitspopany Press, 2001. ISBN: 1930143125.**

After Pharaoh has managed to rid his palace of all the frogs, the littlest frog might just be able to convince him to change his mind and free the Jewish slaves. Playful, humorous rhymes are sure to be a crowd pleaser, especially with the addition of a frog prop and combined with the singing of the familiar song: "One morning when Pharaoh awoke in his bed, there were frogs on his bed and frogs on his head. Frogs on his nose and frogs on his toes. Frogs here, frogs there, frogs are jumping everywhere!"

Sasso, Sandy Eisenberg. *In God's Name.* **Illustrated by Phoebe Stone. Woodstock, VT: Jewish Lights Publishing, 1994. ISBN 1879045265.**

People of different ages, backgrounds, and professions each call God by a different name, like "Shepherd," "Healer," and "Source of Light." They argue about which is the real name for God until at the end they all say their names for God together and then call God "One."

Silverman, Erica. *Raisel's Riddle.* **Illustrated by Susan Gaber. New York: Farrar, Straus and Giroux, 1999. ISBN: 0374361681.**

In this twist on the Cinderella story, Raisel, a poor, orphan girl, wins the heart and mind of the rabbi's son using the teachings from the Talmud that she learned from her beloved grandfather.

Terwilliger, Kelly. *Bubbe Isabella and the Sukkot Cake.* **Illustrated by Phyllis Hornung. Minneapolis: Kar-Ben Publishing, 2005. ISBN 9781580131872.**

Each night Bubbe Isabella wishes for someone to sit with her in her sukkah and share her freshly baked lemon cake. However, the only guests she receives are animals until a young boy arrives looking for a flag for Simchat Torah. This unique story connects the holidays of Sukkot and Simchat Torah, and the simple text and repetitive plot read well aloud.

Vorst, Rochel Groner. *The Sukkah That I Built.* **Illustrated by Liz Victor-Elsby. Brooklyn: Hachai Publishing, 2002. ISBN: 1929628072.**

In this cumulative rhyme story, a young boy describes the sukkah that he assembles with the help of his family.

Zemach, Margot. *It Could Always Be Worse.* **New York: Sunburst; 1990. ISBN: 0374436363 (reissue).**

This is perhaps the best retelling of the familiar Eastern European Jewish folktale featuring a poor man who lives in a crowded house. When he solicits the rabbi's advice, he finds himself with a house full of animals. Only after the animals go back outside does the family realize how peaceful, quiet, clean, and spacious their house is after all. Other versions of the story include *Could Anything Be Worse?* by Marilyn Hirsh, *The Rabbi's Wisdom* by Erica Gordon, *A Big Quiet House* by Heather Forest, *Terrible, Terrible!* by Robin Bernstein, and *The Little, Little House* by Jessica Souhami.

Recommended Books to Retell during Tot Shabbat

When used in a large group setting, these wonderful stories are better suited for retelling and/or acting out.

Cohen, Barbara. *Yussel's Prayer.* **Illustrated by Michael Deraney. New York: Lothrop, Lee and Shepard Books, 1981. ISBN 068800461X.**

Yussel, a poor, uneducated orphan boy finds a way to express his heartfelt prayers to God through music. See also *Daniel and the Silver Flute* by Gerald C. Ruthen.

Davis, Aubrey. *Bone Button Borscht.* **Illustrated by Dušan Petričić. Toronto: Kids Can Press, 1995. ISBN 1550742248.**

In this variation of the "Stone Soup" story, a beggar teaches an entire town about the joys of working together, sharing, and celebrating as a community with the help of some magical buttons. Using a large soup pot, six buttons, a wooden spoon, a water pitcher, sugar, salt and pepper shakers, a pickle jar, and vegetables (real or plastic), invite participants to add to the borscht as you tell the story.

Herman, Charlotte. *How Yussel Caught the Gefilte Fish.* **Illustrated by Katya Krenina. New York: Dutton Children's Books, 1999. ISBN: 0525454497.**

Yussel is so excited to fish with his father for the first time. Hoping to catch a gefilte fish, he is disappointed when a carp, a trout, and a pike are lured by his challah dough bait. But, with the special spice of Shabbat, Mama is magically able to produce gefilte fish for the Shabbat evening meal.

Hirsh, Marilyn. *Joseph Who Loved the Sabbath.* **Illustrated by Devis Grebu. New York: Viking Kestrel, 1986. ISBN 0670811947.**

Illuminating the Talmudic teaching "He who lends to the Sabbath, the Sabbath repays him," Joseph works hard all week for a greedy and selfish farmer so that he can buy only the finest things for Shabbat.

Klein-Higger, Joni. *Ten Tzedakah Pennies.* **Illustrated by Tova Leff. Brooklyn: HaChai Publishing, 2005. ISBN: 1929628196.**

A young boy has ten pennies, and one by one the members of his family place them in a *tzedakah* box. Create large penny props and act out the story with volunteers from the congregation. The simple, rhyming text can easily be adapted to include children's names. See also *The Very Best Place for a Penny* by Dina Rosenfeld.

Kushner, Lawrence, and Gary Schmidt. *In God's Hands.* **Illustrated by Matthew J. Baek. Woodstock, VT: Jewish Lights Publishing, 2005. ISBN: 1580232248.**

Jacob, a rich man, always falls asleep in synagogue but one day wakes up just in time to hear the words of Leviticus read: "You shall bake twelve loaves of challah, and set them before Me in two rows, six in each row." He is certain that God is talking directly to him, so he hurries home and quickly bakes twelve loaves of bread. He brings them to the synagogue and places them in the ark. David, the poor synagogue caretaker, discovers the loaves and believes that they were sent from God to answer his prayers for food to feed his family. When the rabbi happens upon the two men and reveals to them what has been happening, they both learn how their hands have become God's hands in creating a miracle. Similar to *Bagels from Benny* by Aubrey Davis, this retelling follows the original version more closely and has a slightly more sophisticated message.

Lieberman, Syd. *The Wise Shoemaker of Studena.* **Illustrated by Martin Lemelman. Philadelphia: Jewish Publication Society, 1994. ISBN: 0827605099.**

Yossi, a wise and gentle shoemaker, is invited to the home of one of the wealthiest merchants. After a muddy mishap, Yossi is mistaken for a beggar. He returns dressed in fine, distinguished clothes and attempts to teach the partygoers a lesson in hospitality. Act out the story by wearing a large overcoat and feeding it wine, soup, peas, carrots, chicken, dessert, and tea.

Rothenberg, Joan. *Yettele's Feathers*. New York: Hyperion Books for Children, 1995. ISBN: 0786800976.

Yettele enjoys spreading stories about her neighbors, never paying attention to their accuracy. To teach her a lesson about the power of words, the rabbi tells her to put a feather on every doorstep in town and then instructs her to gather them up again. Act out the story by distributing feathers to the congregation. See also *A Sack Full of Feathers* by Debby Waldman.

Schwartz, Howard. *Before You Were Born*. Illustrated by Kristina Swarner. Brookfield, CT: Roaring Brook Press, 2005. ISBN: 1596430281.

Noted storyteller Howard Schwartz retells the midrash of the angel Lailah and provides an explanation for why each one of us has an indentation on our upper lip.

Story Collections

For more ideas, consult one of the many collections of Jewish stories available.

Fisher, Adam. *God's Garden: Children's Stories Grown from the Bible*. Springfield, NJ: Behrman House, 1999. ISBN: 0874416965.

Includes forty-six original stories to complement the weekly *parashah*, with suggestions of props and ideas for dramatizing the story.

Gellman, Marc. *Does God Have a Big Toe? Stories about Stories in the Bible*. Illustrated by Oscar de Mejo. New York: Harper & Row, 1989. ISBN: 0060224320.

A collection of short, funny stories that connect to many of the stories found in Genesis and Exodus. See also *God's Mailbox: More Stories about Stories in the Bible*.

Goldreich, Gloria. *Ten Traditional Jewish Children's Stories*. Illustrated by Jeffrey Allon. New York: Pitspopany Press, 1996. ISBN: 0943706696.

Ten traditional stories are succinctly retold in accessible language; also includes discussion questions for each story. See also *Ten Best Jewish Children's Stories, Ten Classic Jewish Children's Stories*, and *Ten Holiday Jewish Children's Stories*.

Maisel, Grace Ragues, and Samantha Shubert. *A Year of Jewish Stories*. Illustrated by Tammy L. Keiser. New York: URJ Press, 2004. ISBN: 9780807408957.

Fifty-two stories drawn from the Bible, Talmud, midrash, and folklore, one for each week of the year.

Oberman, Sheldon. *Solomon and the Ant and Other Jewish Folktales*. Hondesdale, PA: Boyds Mills Press, 2006. ISBN: 1590783077.

This is a thoroughly enjoyable collection of diverse Jewish folktales that will make excellent read-alouds and will delight audiences of all ages.

Rosman, Steven M. *The Bird of Paradise and Other Sabbath Stories.* Illustrated by Joel Iskowitz. New York: UAHC Press, 1994. ISBN 0807405299.

A great resource if you are looking to connect your Tot Shabbat story with the weekly Torah portion; the stories in this collection are organized by *parashah.* (Note: This book is out of print but can be found in many synagogue libraries and private collections.)

Schram, Peninnah. *Chosen Tales: Stories Told by Jewish Storytellers.* Northvale, NJ: Jason Aronson, 1995. ISBN 1568213522.

"The Apple Tree's Discovery" (pp. 3–4) is a perfect story for Tot Shabbat, especially if you retell it with large props: make a large red apple out of paper, a second apple that is sliced in the middle to show the seeds shaped in a star, and a tinfoil knife. Also recommended: "The Rest of Creation" (pp. 398–399).[1] See also *Jewish Stories One Generation Tells Another* and *The Hungry Clothes and Other Jewish Folktales.*

Schwartz, Howard, and Barbara Rush. *A Coat for the Moon and Other Jewish Tales.* Illustrated by Michael Iofin. Philadelphia: Jewish Publication Society, 1999. ISBN: 082760596X.

A collection of fifteen classic Jewish folktales from around the world with source notes and commentary. Master storyteller Howard Schwartz has edited numerous collections, including *The Diamond Tree* and *The Wonder Child.*

Invaluable Resources

Elswit, Sharon Barcan. *Jewish Story Finder: A Guide to 363 Tales Listing Subjects and Sources.* Jefferson, NC: McFarland & Company, 2005. ISBN: 0786421924.

Are you looking for a story on a specific theme or subject? Do you remember hearing a wonderful story but don't know where to find it? This book can help! Hundreds of stories are indexed by title and subject, and each entry includes a summary, subjects, and a listing of different versions of the story with their sources.

Silver, Linda R. *Jewish Values Finder: A Guide to Values in Jewish Children's Literature.* New York: Neal Schuman Publishers, 2007. ISBN: 155570624X.

Still can't find the perfect book? Turn to this reference guide or go to www.ajljewishvalues.org for a listing of nearly one thousand carefully selected children's books that promote Jewish values. Each entry includes an annotation, age-level recommendations, subject headings, and relevant Jewish values. From the Web site, you can search the database by title, author, subject, or value and narrow your search by age level.

---

[1] Suggested by Enid Kent Sperber, Librarian, Temple Israel of Hollywood (Los Angeles, CA).

Part V

How Can
Tot Shabbat
Be Enhanced?

13

Make It Musical

Carol Boyd Leon

When it comes to Tot Shabbat, music functions as the mortar that holds the service together. It acts to keep little ones focused and interested as you move from one part of the service to the next. But music can be more. In fact, music can be not only the mortar but the bricks as well!

A Tot Shabbat service that is conducted as a service-in-song has the power to be thoroughly enjoyable, uplifting, and enlightening. A song-filled service can be a worshipful and participatory service for both the children and their parents. No matter what emotional state the families enter with, they inevitably leave smiling. With a song-filled service, they'll feel refreshed, thankful, and confident that they began or continued Shabbat in precisely the right way.

A Few Basic Q&As

Does it take a world-class voice to lead a musical Tot Shabbat service?

No. But it takes someone who can naturally, comfortably, and convincingly convey the joy of Jewish prayer and song.

Can one person do it alone?

Yes. But two or more people can combine their efforts to lead the children and their family members in prayer and song.

Is it necessary to use a musical instrument?

No. A guitar or a piano or another accompaniment instrument injects some extra *ruach* into the service. But you can do the same with your enthusiasm. In fact, I often alternate singing with guitar and without so that I can have my hands free to lead hand motions or American Sign Language, hand out props, carry the Torah, and so on. I find that variety goes a long way in helping children stay focused, so I purposely accompany most songs but also lead one or two without accompaniment.

How about singing along to recorded music?

Singing along to recorded music at services can feel very stilted and reduce the likelihood that congregants will sing along. Singing on occasion to an instrumental recording might add variety to an otherwise a cappella service.

What about giving instruments to children?

Great idea! Kids will love it! I always provide tambourines and shakers to create a "*Mi Chamochah* band." But then we collect the instruments, and I make a point of reminding the children that we can pray with song and dance and instruments and we can also pray without even making a sound. What makes the rhythm instruments so special is that they are not used throughout the entire service. Choose the instruments carefully so they're safe for little ones, fun to play, and not so loud as to overwhelm the song itself.

Should the music at each Tot Shabbat be the same?

Children, just like most adults, like consistency and are comfortable with what feels familiar to them—but they're also challenged by what's new to them. The new sometimes causes them to listen harder and think longer about the lyrics. So while the bulk of the music at my Tot Shabbat services is the same from one service to the next, for a few prayers I may choose between a couple of melodies (which, after a few services, also become familiar). But I usually toss in something brand new or sung perhaps just once a year. It keeps us all on our toes—thinking, learning, reacting.

Is it possible to be too "upbeat"?

I love smiles. I want Tot Shabbat to be a happy time for everyone who is there. I want it truly to be a celebration of Shabbat. I make sure the children have plenty of chances to express their joy by moving and dancing and marching. On balance, I sincerely want it to be an upbeat service. But that doesn't mean there shouldn't be quiet moments, peaceful moments, even somewhat introspective moments. And I do think Tot Shabbat should *not* be essentially a nonstop dance party, a children's concert, or a movement-and-music class. Those are all wonderful activities for young children. But they're not the same as a worship service.

What should I do about adults who are talking while I'm song leading?

Try to prevent that situation from occurring. Have children sit with parents. Let parents know they are their children's role models. Make it known that Tot Shabbat is a service for families to enjoy together, rather than for children to attend essentially alone while adults sit apart from them. Be sure to build in moments when children and parents interact. For instance, you may want to begin the *V'ahavta* by asking congregants to give a hug to someone they love. Have children and parents together dance the hora. Ask parents to place a hand on their child's head during the blessing of the children. Using these techniques, parents will realize that their active participation is both desired and important.

Keep It "Singable"

Songs that are "singable" have the following:

- A limited range (less than an octave)
- A limited number of words

- Some repetition of lyrics
- A generally straightforward, somewhat predictable (but still lovely) melody
- A rhythm that's not overly complex

In addition, songs that have a built-in echo are very congregant-friendly, particularly for young children. Incidentally, songs without a built-in echo can still be taught in a listen-and-repeat manner. Simply sing a phrase and ask the children and their family members to sing it back to you.

Equally important is the key of the song, which fortunately is something over which a service leader or song leader has control. Many people mistakenly believe that to sing with children, it's necessary to sing "up high." However, most children match pitches best when they're not especially high. You'll find that songs that use the notes C-D-E-F-G will indeed be sung the most easily, accurately, and comfortably.

Of course, you'll need to find a key that you, as the leader of the music, can comfortably sing. But to encourage others to sing with you, try to stay away from your highest notes if you're a soprano or tenor and your lowest notes if you're an alto or bass.

Remember to sing clearly and enunciate. This is not a voice recital; at Tot Shabbat, simple is best. Even if you seek songs with fairly simple lyrics, some of the words you sing undoubtedly will be new to a few of the children. Be creative in how you help them understand the meaning of the lyrics—showing a picture, offering a brief explanation or asking older children to volunteer one, and providing examples from familiar stories are all methods of giving meaning to unfamiliar words.

You'll undoubtedly find that some of the little ones are not yet singing or even talking, but you can still involve them in the music by making it interactive—stretching up high to the heavens, putting a hand on their heart, clapping hands, singing, marching, dancing, keeping the rhythm on their knees, even showing their muscles during the singing of an abbreviated *V'ahavta* ("with all their strength"). The possibilities for musical involvement are almost limitless.

Be Choosey When Choosing Repertoire

All aspects of a Tot Shabbat service, including the music, should be child-friendly. That doesn't mean, however, that all the music needs to be exclusively "children's music." Some of the simpler songs regularly sung by your congregation can and should be integrated successfully into Tot Shabbat. Some examples of this are the *Sh'ma, Bar'chu,* or perhaps a *nigun* that is sung every week.

It is important to become familiar with the melodic possibilities. Then choose what you feel best fits the mood of the prayer, meets the criteria for "singability" by young children, and is something you'll feel comfortable songleading.

I like to vary the styles, tempos, and moods from song to song, and sometimes even within the same song or prayer. I'll move from a sweet, lullaby-like *V'ahavta* to a lively, celebratory *Mi Chamochah*. I'll often sing an *Oseh Shalom* that starts slow and quiet but eventually becomes like a hora, encouraging families to get and up dance.

I try to integrate at least a few "congregational melodies," but I feel comfortable including many songs that are unique to Tot Shabbat. Young people have an amazing capacity to learn an almost limitless number of melodies, and so I don't feel that all the melodies used at the "big people's services" need to find their way into Tot Shabbat. Yes, we eventually want our children to feel at home in those "big people's services," but more importantly, I want them to feel at home at Tot Shabbat services. So I choose music that I believe will speak to them.

For a song to do that, children need to know what they're singing. So I often sing prayers in both English and Hebrew. Or I explain in advance—in just a few words—the meaning of the Hebrew song or prayer. In fact, before we sing the *Bar'chu*, I use the "traditional" (Solomon Sulzer) *Bar'chu* melody to sing these instructions:

> Please stand up and then I'll ask if you're ready to pray.
> You'll answer by praising God to whom our praise is due.

"Traditional" melodies, folk tunes, songs of Israeli origin, Chasidic songs, music of contemporary Jewish American composers—you may find a place for all of these and more in your services. Some Tot Shabbat leaders write their own songs for services, and others write new lyrics to existing melodies. With a creative song leader or service leader, the possibilities are endless.

Go Sparingly on Parody Songs

Melodies are designed to evoke certain emotions and memories. When I hear the Chanukah candle blessing sung, I think of latkes and chocolate gelt, of my childhood and those of my own grown children. But when I hear someone using that same melody to light the Shabbat candles, I feel unsettled.

The same thing happens when I hear children being taught a song about summertime or *tzedakah* or Passover with lyrics set to the melody of "I Have A Little Dreidel."

Sure, many teachers and song leaders find it's easy to take a familiar melody, whether the dreidel song or "Twinkle, Twinkle, Little Star" or any of a dozen other nursery rhymes, and create Shabbat lyrics for it. This eliminates the effort required to learn and teach a new melody. But I think we do our children a disservice if we teach them umpteen sets of lyrics to just a few melodies; doing so prevents those melodies from evoking a particular feeling and robs the children of the opportunity to expand their musical horizons. The disadvantage of doing so is compounded when the new lyrics are in such stark contrast to the original focus of the song—say, using "If You're Happy and You Know It" for a Passover song about Pharaoh's treatment of the Israelites—that it completely confuses the children. Occasionally using the "If You're Happy" melody for a song about being happy on Shabbat, however, could add a touch of fun to your service.

We often sing parodies at Purim because we aim for the fun factor, such as using the "Bingo" melody to spell H-A-M-A-N. In fact, entire Purim-spiels are often created by rewriting the lyrics of Broadway musicals. It's often the surprise of hearing special Purim lyrics take the place of the words we were expecting that makes Purim so much fun. It's purposeful confusion.

However, Tot Shabbat isn't the place for such confusion (nor for sarcasm, which can so easily be misunderstood). There is such a wealth of wonderful Jewish music written specifically to teach about Shabbat and our other holidays, our values, our traditions, and the teachings of Torah that I urge service and song leaders to save the parodies for Purim and expand their repertoire of Jewish music.

The Pros and Cons of Spontaneity

Being an effective song leader may include the ability to switch gears when something isn't working or to change some song choices when the children at the service turn out to be younger or older than you were expecting. For some song leaders, however, spontaneity in music choices isn't a viable option because their discomfort at switching gears in the middle of a service would be too evident. Chances are, the more experienced they become at leading Tot Shabbat music, however, the more comfortable they will be with making some spontaneous choices based on the mood and ages of the children who are present.

At the very least, every song leader can figure out how to shorten a song that isn't working. One suggestion is to have at least a couple of melody choices in your service binder for some of the prayers so you have choices at hand.

"Zipper songs" are those that include an opportunity to fill in the blank with a spontaneous word or phrase provided live by a child. For instance, you might ask children for special things they like to do on Shabbat or for places where they feel God's presence and include their suggestions in a song. Song leaders successfully use zipper songs to turn children into active participants and to give children some ownership of the music.

Please note, however, that children are unpredictable, and you can't know in advance all the ways they'll suggest you fill in the blank. I am much more apt to use zipper songs in classroom settings where it's generally not a problem to explain why a particular response (such as one that's off-color) is inappropriate. I prefer not risking such responses at services, and so I tend to steer clear of zipper songs at Tot Shabbat.

Singing It with Song Sheets

When I first started leading Tot Shabbat services in the 1990s, I created a service booklet for each service that included a sentence of introduction to each prayer as well as the words to each prayer and song. Many parents liked these booklets, but they were of no benefit to the children (except for a few older, reading-age siblings). In fact, the booklets got in the way when it came to clapping hands, giving hugs, dancing, marching with plush Torahs, and more. And I came to realize that an overly scripted Tot Shabbat was too static and inflexible.

I recommend making song sheets available. Adults who aren't familiar with the songs and prayers will appreciate them, and it's important for parents and grandparents to feel comfortable if you want them to keep bringing their children to services. You can customize the song sheet for particular services by adding the lyrics to any special holiday songs or *parashah*-based songs you're planning to include that week.

But keep in mind that song sheets are of no value to the vast majority of children at Tot Shabbat services. Your method of leading and teaching music should not rely on a song sheet; rather, the songs need to be accessible to pre-readers.

More Ways—Mainly Musical—to Keep Children Involved

When families attend one of my Tot Shabbat services for the first time, they're often astounded that their child "lasted" from beginning to end—which means at least fifty minutes of rapt listening by children too young to talk or sing. I give music 90 percent of the credit. The service-in-song model does most of the work for you. But following are some of the additional techniques I use to keep the children involved:

1. Upon entering the room, each of the children chooses a color-coded, graphic, laminated "helper card" that lets them (and me!) know how they'll help during the service:
   - "Symbols of Shabbat" helpers—candles, candlesticks, *Kiddush* cup, challot, challah cover—take those items from a little Shabbat table and hold them up for everyone to see during the singing of "Shalom Shabbat Shalom," a song that lets the children practice the three blessings (even if it's Saturday morning, when we wouldn't be lighting candles).
   - "Musicians" play tambourines during *Mi Chamochah* (although I generally have bells and shakers for other children to play).
   - "Torah helpers" open and close the ark, march with the child-size Torah from which I read (all the other children march with a similar-size plush Torah), undress and dress the Torah, and "help" me hold the *yad*.
   - "CPOs"—challah passer-outers!—take challah in baskets to all the congregants at the end of the service.
   - "It's my birthday month!" helpers hold the *Kiddush* cup (I bring a few extras to accommodate all who are celebrating a birthday that month) and help lead the *Kiddush* and *HaMotzi* at the conclusion of the service.
   - "Bim-bammers" lead the way to the *Oneg Shabbat* as we sing "Bim Bam/Shabbat Shalom" or "Shalom Aleichem, Peace to Us."
2. All children march with plush Torahs at the start of the Torah service as we sing "Torah, Torah" and other Torah songs.
3. Children sitting farther back are invited to come up close before I start to tell a story that generally reinforces a lesson from the line or two I've read from the Torah. They help with sound effects (e.g., animal sounds

or wind) and often volunteer answers to questions I ask during the course of the story.

4. Children gather under a giant tallit whose corners are held up high by four adults for the traditional Shabbat blessing of the children, including a sung *Y'varech'cha*.

5. The children and I "dance our thanks" to a lively rendition of a song that gives thanks to God.

Ready, Set, SING!

Ready . . . To be a confident leader of songs, put in the time it takes to get yourself ready. Learn the music well; the service itself isn't the place to introduce music that you are still learning. Getting ready also includes making certain that your accompaniment instrument, if you use one, is in good condition and in tune and that you have prepared your service binder and included in it any special songs and stories for the week.

Set . . . Remember to warm up your voice before the service. Then make sure the room is set up as you need it, starting with the congregants' seating. I like wide, U-shaped rows with plenty of room between the rows and a center aisle for easy access. Make sure there's room up front or wherever you plan for dancing to take place. Be sure you have what you need to allow the service to progress smoothly.

Do you need a Torah reading table and candlelighting or Shabbat symbols table? Is there a music stand or lectern for your use? But don't get into the rut of being tied to the music stand or lectern. Vary your location to help establish both eye contact and smile contact with each child, as well as to demonstrate movements, tell an animated story, march with the Torah, and so on. Weather permitting, I hold some Tot Shabbat services outdoors in a clearing in the woods. The birds sing with us as we take the Torahs on a song-filled nature walk along a path through the woods.

If possible, you're likely to benefit from a sound system that includes a wireless headset or lapel mini-microphone so you're not tied to a stationary microphone. It is important for congregants young and old alike not to have to strain to hear you, and with young children, you never can be sure how much "background noise" will be competing with your voice. If you have a small group or are in a small space, no amplification is needed. If you have a big group or are in a big room, a wireless system is ideal, but a microphone with a long cord can also be workable. I even set up a portable sound system for outdoor services.

Sing! Set inhibitions aside. Let your own inner light shine. Sing with an open heart. By doing so, you'll help Shabbat find a place in the hearts of those with whom you worship.

I hope this chapter, along with the others in this guide, inspires you to create your own musical Tot Shabbat service. By sharing the joy that music brings you, you'll have it returned over and over again through the Shabbat smiles of those whom you are privileged to lead.

14

Puppets on the Pulpit

Marilyn Price

The best learning of all, say the best educators of all, comes from stories. The best storytelling for the youngest (and in most cases even the not so young) are stories with a visual aid. Puppets are the best visual aid. They add a lifelike perspective to the drama of the story, add a focus point and an opportunity to stretch imaginations, and create connections beyond just the word of the moment and into the everyday experience. In fact, puppets have a magic all their own, and well used, they multiply the manipulator's skills.

Puppets have been around for over three thousand years. Initially used in religious ceremonies, the oldest of them were used to enhance the stories and ceremonies in many cultures, and that practice continues today. There are several skilled ways that puppetry can be used in the Tot Shabbat experience.

Fear of Puppets
(Or Rather, Fear of Looking Foolish with Puppets)

I was first asked to do a puppet show thirty-eight years ago by a girlfriend in my synagogue. I laughed out loud. At the time I was a management consultant for a worldwide corporation, and it seemed like a ridiculous idea—I moved people across a factory in the quickest amount of time, not puppets! But I was pregnant, and she was a good friend. The first time I put a puppet on my hand I realized that I had found my medium. I was in charge! The puppets always do what I tell them. (Keep that in mind. It helps.)

It isn't fear of puppets that many of us feel, but rather, fear of looking foolish. Many adults are intimidated by a piece of cloth or other material that has the power to make the most skillful professionals feel as if they look ridiculous, so they don't use this art form. With that in mind, let me remind you of the prize at the end of the day. Puppets work, and no one will think you look foolish. Children will love you for using them, and parents will be inspired.

The quickest way to become proficient in puppetry is to rehearse. Practice with this actor or actress you are involving in the story or the activity. I recommend finding a quiet space alone, putting the character on your hand or holding the object that is being used, and integrating it into the text of your service without an audience. After you are comfortable with physically holding the character, using whichever hand is best, you should place it in a box in front of you, in a pocket, or behind a prayer book for a dramatic entry. (I always recommend a dramatic entry, even if it's from a bag or a box; if the puppet has a recognizable home that is in plain sight, the community will know that it is coming, and anticipation will add to the drama.) Then practice what the puppet is going to say or do. The voice of the puppet should be your voice at first. No one will care. The stress of maintaining a special voice is unnecessary, and generally voices used by "not yet ready for prime time puppeteers" are silly. If you are beyond that phase, forgive me. Here, however, is the simplest way to become proficient and comfortable in your puppetry. Watch the puppet at work as you would watch a friend. When the puppet speaks or moves, look at it. In turn, when you speak or you ask someone else to speak, have the puppet look at you and then at the other person. It is a most effective tool.

The Shabbat Starter Puppet

For the novice puppeteer I recommend starting simply, with one character used for a particular purpose. Let's begin with the puppet cantor, for example, a puppet that starts the *nigun*. This is easy because you don't have to teach the puppet words nor do you have to know many. The puppet can lead the community in song, be moved around easily, and be in total harmony with the puppeteer. The puppet can be a manufactured hand puppet, a musical instrument made "puppetlike" with eyeballs, a box with a hole cut in the front like a guitar personified with a face, or a puppet made specifically for that purpose with a pattern available in a resource kit.

Within the context of the Tot Shabbat service, there are many opportunities to expand the puppets' roles. One possibility is a puppet responsible for listening skills. This could be your very own *Sh'ma* puppet. Explain that whenever *Sh'ma* appears (and yes, I would call the character *Sh'ma*) that means listening is required. *Sh'ma* never needs to speak; *Sh'ma* just listens. Whenever *Sh'ma* appears, the kids will know that the time has come to listen.

The Torah service offers a variety of opportunities for using puppets. A puppet could narrate the *parashah*, be an interactive part in the telling, or be the *yad* or the one who "points" out the pivotal value in the story. You can create some principal characters for the Torah stories, which might include the matriarchs and patriarchs, Moses, Miriam, Adam, Eve, or some notable animal friends (an amiable camel or a knowledgeable, well-herded sheep), to carry the stories along and act as an interpreter. You might consider manufacturing (or purchasing) a box of available puppets or dolls that will help tell the story with volunteer or appointed hands.

Parental involvement is a key aspect of Tot Shabbat, and puppets can be a great way to get parents involved. I realize that most parents are delighted to bring the kids to services and totally unprepared to learn anything themselves. We need to honor their presence and use it. I would recommend finding a role

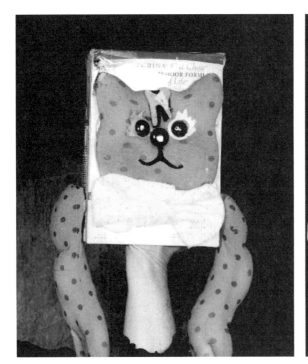

Cat on the hand!

Couldn't be easier or moooo fun.

for them that will increase their own knowledge and make them teachers for their children. One way is to make them responsible for the family of puppets in your space. We often parcel out musical instruments to the kids but rarely to the parents; the same is usually true of puppets. Try handing out your resources of physical characters or props to enhance the story for the adults and the children alike. It is my general rule that if you are giving a puppet a larger role that requires some teaching, as opposed to just sounds, then give the puppet to a willing adult. The best would be if you have a set, and that should go to one family. Don't leave out a sibling, if at all possible.

I also recommend only handing out the hardiest of puppets, so that you need not worry about the puppets' physical condition, and just a few at a time so that the flow of the service is smoother. If you have an opportunity to do this before the service, it is even better.

Puppets should be given rules before they go into the community. I always teach my youngest puppeteers that puppets are for stories and peaceful play. No fighting! You can announce the rules as you hand the puppets out and commend the children (and the puppets) on their behavior when they return the puppets.

Another great Tot Shabbat experience is to create a time within the service for the parents to talk about the week with their kids (what went right, what went wrong, how to honor that and then bless the week and let it move on). It is a habit-forming exercise and need not be shared with the community but done as a family, and then the community of families can pray together. You could model that with a puppet family that will turn the time over to the group.

Tot Shabbat is not a great time to create puppets, but at another time it would be terrific to help your families design and make puppets to have on hand (pun intended). Understanding that total participation will generally not happen, there is much to be said for the interested people becoming the foundation of the experience, so that others may then follow. Easily made characters and recyclable objects made into characters will not only enhance the participants' experience but will create wonderful entries into friendships that constant community participation can provide.

Examples might be animals, such as cows from milk cartons or cats from cat food boxes. Tot Shabbat family regulars can also make puppets from their favorite food boxes with their photo images pasted on the front. They are easy to make and sit politely around the room!

Integrating the self-made puppet into the story teaches and enriches the experience in many ways. There is no good reason that you can't have a cat in most stories (certainly they have been around long enough), and cows are mentioned many times in the Torah.

There are many opportunities to stretch the leader's own imagination and enhance the experience not only for the gathered community but for service leaders as well. Clearly, as in all new skills, there should be some time allowed for practice. A thing not done well is not worth doing. But puppets have a magic all their own and represent an easily attained new skill set. They create ways for the smallest of kids to focus and concentrate. They give adults the opportunity to become engaged in their children's responses and to become the teachers we help them to be. Everybody loves a puppet even if they don't know it!

15

Using the *Torah Alive!* Curriculum to Teach *Parashat HaShavua* in a Tot Shabbat Setting

Lorraine Posner Arcus

Young children love stories. The Torah, God's great gift to the Jewish people, is our great book of amazing stories. It is filled with wonderful lessons, exciting personalities, and enthralling events. Torah study for young children should be vibrant and exciting, capitalizing on their love of lessons taught in "story" form. Through the study of Torah, the children learn a set of relevant values and are provided with the opportunity to discuss sensitive feelings and issues. *Torah Alive!* (URJ Press, 2004), the curriculum and method of teaching Torah that is described in this chapter, is based on developmentally appropriate experiences for young children and my personal experiences in the early childhood classroom.

Children learn by doing. The children readily identify with the biblical figures and the Torah comes alive as the children become active participants in the weekly Torah lessons. By re-creating the lessons from the Torah through their own dramatization, young students make it their own. If we imbue in our children a love of Torah study and enhance their learning with pictorial and artistic representations of the Torah lesson, the children are likely to develop a sense of the Torah as an integral part of their everyday lives.

The Torah: Sacred Words

As preparation for embarking on Torah study, you may teach about the physical qualities of the Torah: the *atzei chayim* (Torah rollers), the parchment, how a Torah is written, who writes a Torah, the *rimonim* (Torah crowns), when the Torah is read, where the Torah is kept, the differences between a Sephardic Torah and an Ashkenazic Torah. It is very exciting for children to see a "real" *sefer Torah*. It would be wonderful to have a small *sefer Torah* (real or stuffed!) in your prayer space.

The Setting: Sacred Space

If possible, designate a space in your prayer space to be used consistently for Torah study. Just as the Torah has its own special place in the *aron kodesh* within the synagogue, the study of Torah has its own place within your room. This might mean bringing the children up onto the bimah or having them sit on the floor at the leader's feet, instead of in the chairs with their parents. Changing seating or spaces gives the children the sense that something special is coming. Moving also helps with any "itchiness."

The Lesson: Sacred Time

If you're using this method for presenting each new weekly *parashah*, before each Shabbat you must examine the *parashah* for a lesson to which the children can relate and find relevance. There are some *parashiyot* that can present quite a challenge! Alternatively, if you're presenting highlights of Torah lessons, you will have more latitude in choosing themes and lessons and may spend several weeks on particular lessons that appear to be more exciting and relevant to young children.

Before dramatizing the lesson, you may want to provide a brief introduction to the story so the children can create a scene using their own imagination. Storytelling is an ancient Jewish custom. Capitalize on its magic when relating the lessons of the Torah to the children. Presentation of the actual Torah story may take only five minutes. However, if time allows it, you may take more time to do things like putting on costumes, creating a backdrop and scenery, and discussing relevant questions.

Some lessons may invite all children (or adults!) to wear costumes. At other times, the participants will take turns being part of the audience or dressing as a Torah personality, always being reassured that they will get a turn soon. Young children generally love to "dress up." Catch the excitement as they role-play as these ancient and interesting personalities.

For purposes of dramatizing the lesson, you will be the narrator or facilitator of the story. This will ensure that the children are hearing the story as true to the text as possible. After reviewing the appropriate materials and gathering the necessary costumes, scenery, props, and so on, you will help the children dress as specific personalities and bring the individuals into the scene as the story unfolds. Obviously, if you have a very short amount of time for this part of the service, you will want to keep the costumes and props simple. This can also be done without costumes and props, of course. It is amazing however, just how much a few simple props and/or costumes can add to the creativity of the process and the children's experience. As the story is told, the children will follow the action in mime and movement. You may elicit dialogue through prompting, questioning, and directing. Generally, however, you will need to recite all speaking parts, touching or looking at the person who would be doing the speaking.

Questions: Sacred Discussion

After presenting the dramatization, invite the children to ask their own questions. Young children are regarded by theologians as being some of the best students of Torah. Invite them to offer their interpretations. The open-ended discussions conducted at this age will be an introduction to the way Torah study is conducted throughout one's life. Create an atmosphere in which Torah study is an exploration and discussion, not just storytelling. Encourage the children to question and ponder the lessons from the Torah. When developing your own set of questions, be sure to include ones that are open-ended, sparking curiosity and critical thought, along with those questions that recall facts. Try to be accepting of all children's ideas. There are students and scholars who spend their lives discussing and answering some of these questions. If a child's response appears to be totally off base, you might answer, "That's an interesting point. Does anyone have a different idea?" You can then proceed to have further discussion on an answer that appears to be more reasonable.

"Did This Really Happen?"

Often, the children will ask, "Did this really happen?" A simple and accurate answer would be, "This is how it is written in the Torah." Every Torah is exactly the same. From this text we learn lessons and values that guide our lives. It is important to recognize that Jewish tradition doesn't portray any individual as being exclusively good. The personalities in the Bible were subject to human frailties, made mistakes, and may have used questionable judgment. We acknowledge their mistakes and learn from them. Additionally, the events in the lives of these biblical characters illustrate that despite making mistakes, a person can still travel in the path of God.

Costumes and Head Coverings

The events in the Torah take place in a very warm part of the world, in the region of the Middle East. In ancient times, both men and women wore long robes and covered their heads for protection from the sun and perhaps for reasons of modesty. People of greater prosperity wore more ornate clothing. Fabrics were dyed with natural materials and may have been very bright and colorful. Each time the children are dressed as the personalities from the Torah, they may wear long robes and a head covering. The matriarchs and patriarchs, our leaders, may have been dressed in more ornate clothing.

For "furry" costumes, fleece, terry cloth, velour fabrics, or the old fur lining to a coat works well. For animal costumes, fabric stores generally carry a selection of fabric designed to look like the skin of various animals.

Ask parents and caregivers to bring old bathrobes, large T-shirts, fabric yardage, and so on. These can all be cut to size for the children. You can fashion these into long robes and embellish them with trim, sequins, or small pieces of fabric using craft glue or hot glue.

Head coverings are easily fashioned from old T-shirts. Holding the T-shirt by its arms, first wrap the top of the T-shirt around the front of the child's forehead, with the "body" of the T-shirt draping down toward the child's back. Secure the head covering by bringing the arms around to the back of the child's head and tie them in a knot. By cutting the front from the back of one T-shirt, two head coverings can be fashioned. Each of the children can store their own head covering in a plastic bag for use each week. Just **wearing** a head covering will transport the child to another place and time. Alternative head coverings can be fashioned from a piece of fabric placed on the child's head and secured with another strip of fabric or elastic.

Men in the time of the Torah probably had beards. You can purchase a beard at a party store or fashion one from furry fabric affixed with elastic. Use a brown or black beard for a young man and a gray or white beard as the personalities "age."

Scenery and Props

By using a backdrop that might resemble the scenery of the lessons from the Torah, the children are able to visualize the setting. Backdrops can be switched or embellished for each new setting. The children will enjoy making the scenery. Before fashioning a backdrop, you can discuss with the children what that scene might look like. A white bedsheet can be painted or decorated using markers, or you can invite the children to draw and cut out components of the scenery and affix it to the sheet.

The people of the Torah lived in tents. Ways to fashion a tent would be to drape an old tablecloth or a large piece of fabric over a tall freestanding object, such as an easel; drape it between two room dividers; or hang it from the ceiling or on a wall.

Many of the lessons involve the use of a tree. An old coat rack with attached leaves will work well. You can fashion a tree from construction paper and affix it to your scenery. Party stores and catalogs sell inflatable and foldable trees as well.

Props are an essential component in some lessons. Many lessons take place at the well, the center of social activity in ancient times. Measure a large piece of paper, plastic, or a shower curtain to go around the outside of a large trashcan. Draw rocks on the paper, or cut them out from gray paper and have the children color or affix them to the larger paper. When needed, wrap the large paper around the can and attach it with tape. Fold and save the "well" paper for future use.

A fire can be made from an open box standing on its short side. Fill the box with yellow and orange tissue paper. Depending on your region and climate, logs and pieces of wood can be used to suggest a campfire.

The Torah and Our Contemporary Lives

Learning Torah is an ongoing process. We study Torah throughout our lives. Each time we learn about a passage or story, even if we have studied it before, we gain new insights, generate new questions, and find new ways to relate those teachings to our everyday lives.

In the course of the year, there will be times when either ordinary or extraordinary events will occur. Seize the opportunity to use teachings from the Torah to solve a problem or relate to something wonderful that has occurred. For example, a guest may come to visit. We learn from Abraham and Sarah how to treat our guests.

Some suggested lessons with specific narrative scripts, including costume, prop, and scenery ideas, as well as related discussion questions, art activities, and supportive materials, can be found in *Torah Alive! An Early Childhood Torah Curriculum* (URJ Press, 2004). Teaching Torah to young children is an exhilarating experience. Enjoy the process, become part of the process, and watch the Torah come **alive**!

Appendix A
Example Formats
and Outlines for Tot Shabbat

Tot Shabbat services can be held at different times (Friday night or Saturday morning). Sometimes they stand alone (usually with an *Oneg Shabbat* or a meal), but sometimes they are part of a larger morning or evening of activities. There is no magic formula, and it may take some trial and error to find out what works best for the young families in your congregation. Once you do figure out what works, it is best to keep the date and time consistent (e.g., the third Friday night of every month).

Example Tot Shabbat Formats

Temple Shalom in Dallas, Texas, holds a Tot Shabbat one Friday night and one Saturday morning each month. On Friday night, they start with the service and then have dinner with an art activity. On Saturday morning, rather than using the weekly Torah portion, they use the URJ's *Torah Alive!* curriculum for the story time (see chapter 15). Their Tot Shabbat service is followed by a *Kiddush*.

At Shir Hadash in Los Gatos, California, Tot Shabbat is held on Saturday mornings using a service booklet of their own creation. Children choose musical instruments and jobs to do. Mask puppets and cuddly Torahs are also part of the service. Leaders take the Torah out and undress it but don't read from it. Afterwards is a *Kiddush* and sometimes a trip to the park.

Congregation Beth Israel in Houston, Texas, offers one Tot Shabbat a month on Friday night, which they call "Tot Shabbat," and one on Saturday morning, which they call "Shabbat Play Date." The congregation meets in a large gym-type room with chairs set up for adults, a rug for kids to sit on, and a portable ark. On Friday night, they do a Tot Shabbat service followed by Shabbat blessings and dinner. The room is set up so that after the children eat, they can run around and play while the parents take more time to eat and talk. On Shabbat morning, there is playtime first, then the Tot Shabbat service, followed by bagels and more playtime.

At Temple Emanuel in Worcester, Massachusetts, the congregation holds a monthly Tot Shabbat on Saturday morning as part of a whole morning of activities called *Yad b'yad*. The morning starts with a Tot Shabbat service, followed by a *Kiddush*. There is a theme for the morning (often the Jewish holiday that is coming up) with a story, songs, art activities, and baking related to the theme.

There are many more examples and models with all kinds of variations. The key is to figure out what will be most successful in your congregation. If something doesn't seem to be working, try something else. Perhaps most importantly, take the time to ask young families what will work for them. You won't be able to accommodate everyone, but you may get a sense of what will work best for the largest number of families.

Example Tot Shabbat Outlines

In the outlines below, submitted by congregations across North America, you will see some similarities and some differences. What they all have in common is that they are a worship service. The core of the traditional worship service is there, although it may be simplified and shortened a great deal. The themes of a service may be represented not by the traditional prayers but in creative and interactive ways. Going beyond the service outline, there are many differences. Some use puppets, some use a lot of music, some have Torah parades, some have Torah readings, while others do not. There are many wonderful, creative approaches to Tot Shabbat and ways to make it a spiritual worship experience for our youngest congregants. Some congregations use "homemade" service booklets as well as *Gates of Prayer for Young Children* (CCAR Press); some, like Treasure Cohen's synagogue, create one large prayer book that sits in front of the congregation and has large pictures to illustrate the themes of the prayers. Some of these outlines are simple, while others are more intricate. Some are simply the order of prayers or list of songs, while others include details about movement, props, and other activities. The outlines are presented as submitted, with minimal editing. The key is for you to develop an outline that you are comfortable with and that works for your community. Keep the ritual and routine, but feel free to try something new too!

Temple Emanu-El, Edison, New Jersey

Submitted by Rabbi Deborah K. Bravo

Kabbalat Shabbat/Songs—These I explain as the warm-ups. We are getting ready for Shabbat. They are our morning stretches. Sometimes we even stretch during this section.

1. *Bar'chu*—This is the call to God, to be sure that God is ready to hear our prayers. Sometimes, using their hands, the children call out to God. I often quiz them on what we need to do at the beginning of the service (call to God).
2. Creation—This is our chance to say thank you to God. We take a moment to allow the children to share their own words of thanks to God. Sometimes they begin each line with *Baruch atah Adonai*. Sometimes

we end with the traditional *chatimah*. Sometimes we sing one of several songs that are great with children for "thank you's" and about creation.

3. Revelation—For this section of the service, we focus both on *Sh'ma* and *V'ahavta*. For *Sh'ma*, I remind them that we believe in one God. They often fill in the blank. We talk about the word *Sh'ma* and what it means. With *V'ahavta*, we discuss the word *oheiv*, and that our best way to show our love for God is by doing mitzvot, and this prayer talks about some of the mitzvot we can do. They often share mitzvot they are doing.

4. Redemption—We typically review the story of freedom from Egypt, and sing and dance to the words of *Mi Chamochah* with great joy and excitement. This is often the time in the service where you can relay something going on in the rest of the world.

5. *T'filah*—This is a difficult decision for a tot service. I often go straight to the silent prayer or focus simply on the *Avot V'Imahot*. We talk about God being the same today, yesterday, and tomorrow, here and everywhere. We sometimes talk about peace and sing *Birkat Shalom*.

6. Torah Service/Story—This is a great opportunity to teach a little bit of Torah ritual, as well as the concept of the weekly portion and what is in it. Here is where the value lesson can be shared.

Temple Sinai, Tenafly, New Jersey

Submitted by Rabbi Jordan Millstein

Opening song or two

Candlelighting

Introduction by rabbi—Ask questions like "Why are we here?" "What does it mean to pray?" "If prayers are special words we say to God, then where is God?" (Pretend to look around the room for God.)

Bar'chu—Before the *Bar'chu*, talk with the children about why we face east.

Sh'ma (with hand motions)

Peter and Ellen Allard's song "Standing at the Sea" with hand motions

Amidah—Ask children what they want to say "thank you" to God for. Get responses.

Torah service—**Short** Torah reading. If space allows, open the Torah and have parents sit holding each end so the children can look into the Torah scroll.

Birthday blessings while the Torah is out

Story

Oseh Shalom (everyone standing with arms around each other—if possible)

Congregation Shir Chadash, Lakewood, California

Submitted by Rabbi Howard O. Laibson

Led with guitar and puppets

Misha Mouse (his name was changed to Mickey at Ellis Island—that's for the parents and grandparents, obviously) welcomes everyone.

Karmit the Frog (complete with *kippah*) says, "Shabbat shalom," and tells everyone that he's really looking forward to leading the "Hebrew Word Song."

Rabbi welcomes everyone.

Sing: "Bim Bam"

Nigun (with the kids snapping fingers or clapping)

"When we come here to temple for this special time, we come to pray to God, because God is very good."

Bar'chu

"Not only is God good, but there is only One God. That's why God is so very special."

Sh'ma

"Hebrew Word Song": Karmit the Frog leads "If you're happy and you know it . . ."

(clap your *yadayim*, stomp your *raglayim*, blink your *einayim*, kiss with your *peh*, etc.). The kids learn how to say many parts of the body in Hebrew.

"God is One, and God is good. And God wants **us** to be good, too. So we sing a prayer that tells us to be good, so that we can all be happy and free."

Mi Chamochah

"What would we all have if everyone was good, happy, and free? **Peace—shalom.**"

Sim Shalom

Torah reading: All Torah ornaments are handed to kids to hold (except the *yad*). Two parents sit in low chairs and hold each end of the Torah (*atzei chayim*) so the children can see the Torah open at their eye level. Read two or three verses from which a brief moral lesson is taught. Then we sing "Al Sh'loshah D'varim" as the children help dress the Torah.

Presentation: The presentation is by another puppet. The Count teaches the kids how to count to three in Hebrew; the Eensie Weensie Achavish leads the song about going up the *mayim* spout, etc. Hebrew words are taught this way.

"And now, as we begin to close our special time together, we sing once more about how very special God is."

Vaanachnu

Oseh Shalom + "Shabbat Shalom"

Cookele (formerly Cookie Monster) leads the *Kiddush* and *HaMotzi*

A Tot Shabbat Service Outline

Submitted by Treasure L. Cohen

Warm-up Shabbat songs

"L'chu N'ran'nah"—"Let Us Rejoice"

Blessing the children

L'chah Dodi—welcoming the Shabbat Queen

Bar'chu—let us bend our knees and worship together

Sh'ma—God is One

Amidah—private prayer—telling God what we are happy about, what we are sad about, what we are excited about, what we are worried about, what we are thankful for . . .

Torah parade

Puppet sermon

Kiddush—blessing over wine

Aleinu—praising God

Announcements by Rabbi Kermit and friends (puppets)

Adon Olam—"Lord of the World"

A Tot Shabbat Service-in-Song Outline

Submitted by Carol Boyd Leon

The ideas listed above are integrated into the following service-in-song. I've included the names of the songwriters whose settings I typically use, but of course you can adapt this outline with your own song and prayer choices.

"Shalom Everyone" (C. B. Leon)

Opening song medley

"Shalom Shabbat Shalom" (C. B. Leon) while children hold symbols of Shabbat

Candle blessing (A. W. Binder) if Friday

"A Special Time," a children's *L'chah Dodi* (C. B. Leon) if Friday

Bar'chu (B. Siegel, after English instructional intro set to S. Sulzer)

Sh'ma (T. Pik or S. Sulzer or "Children's Sh'ma" by C. B. Leon)

"You Shall Love" (C. B. Leon, abbreviated version)

"God Is Everywhere" (P. & E. Allard)

Mi Chamochah (D. Friedman) with tambourines and shakers

Very abbreviated *Amidah*

Silent prayer (with explanation)

Oseh Shalom (N. Hirsch or S. Carlebach, preceded by English *Oseh Shalom* by C. B. Leon) quietly at first, then growing more exuberant

Torah Service:

"Torah, Torah"; "Al Sh'loshah D'varim" (C. Tzur) during *hakafah*

Torah blessings (before and after reading a line or two)

"Tree of Life" (R. Silverman) when returning Torahs to ark

A story (related to the Torah portion or upcoming holiday)

A song or two (related to the story or upcoming holiday)

Blessing under giant tallit: "Birkat Yeladim" (C. B. Leon) or "A Blessing for the Ones You Love" (D. Friedman)

A dance of thanks ("Thank You God" by J. Bowen) and/or song of thanks ("Thank You, Adonai" by C. B. Leon)

Adon Olam (one Hebrew verse, one English verse with echoes) while challah is distributed

Kiddush and *HaMotzi* led by the children celebrating a birthday that month

"Bim Bam/Shabbat Shalom" (N. Frankel) or "Shalom Aleichem, Peace to Us" (C. B. Leon) on way to *Oneg Shabbat* table

Temple Har Zion, Thornhill, Ontario

Submitted by Karen Winkler-Weiss, RJE

Opening songs—"Bim Bam," "Hinei Mah Tov," a *nigun*

"*Baruch atah Adonai*, We thank you so much our God"

(adapted from the morning blessings with movements)

Baruch atah Adonai,

We thank you so much our God,

For giving us . . ."

Eyes to see with Amen

Ears to hear with Amen

Mouths to talk with and sing with Amen

Hands to play with and do our work with Amen

Arms to hug with Amen

Legs to walk, run, and dance with Amen

Bodies to grow with Amen

Sh'ma (we close our eyes and sing slowly)

Mi Chamochah (easy and peppy tune)

Torah service

Hakafah—children come up with tiny Torahs and take musical instruments; one circuit around the sanctuary singing "Torah, Torah"

Story

Closing Song

Candles, *Kiddush*, and *HaMotzi*

Congregation Gates of Prayer, Metairie, Louisiana

Submitted by Rabbi Bob Loewy

Sing—"Bim Bam"

Light candles—say and sing blessing

Kiddush—explain as a toast for Shabbat, say and sing blessing

Talk about Shabbat—time to say blessings, time for families to be together

Parents' blessing—recite and have them hug and kiss children

"Shabbat is a time when we think about God."

Bar'chu—Teach "la, la's" and sing *Bar'chu*

Sh'ma—Sulzer version sung slowly

Mi Chamochah

Talk about Shabbat and Torah—stories that talk about people and God, laws that teach us what to do, help us know what is right and wrong, good or bad

Get Torah while singing "Am Yisrael Chai"

Story—have children come and sit in the well while story is told and acted out

Return Torah while singing "Tree of Life"

Birthday blessings

Concluding song—*Oseh Shalom*

Congregation Beth Israel, Houston, Texas

Submitted by Rabbi Mark Miller

Introduction by the rabbi

Everyone introduces themselves

Three to four fun Shabbat songs

Bar'chu

Sh'ma

"Silent" prayer

Doug Cotler's song "Thank You God"

Appendix B
Tot Shabbat: Taking It Home

Kitty Wolf

In the celebration of Shabbat, the Jewish home is as important as the synagogue. For centuries the home has been where most holiday celebrations occurred and where traditions were passed on from generation to generation. At the very center of the Jewish at-home religious experience is Shabbat.

But for many parents, celebrating Shabbat can be a daunting proposition. They often have little or no experience with home rituals. They feel a time constraint and have saved Saturdays for errands and soccer games. It is important that we give parents encouragement and some tools to take home with them to enable them to continue their Tot Shabbat experience at home. Begin with small steps. Send one or two activities home as a follow-up to the Tot Shabbat program. Stress the importance of making Shabbat different, a day apart, from the other days of the week.

A book list or even the gift of a basic book is a good beginning. Following are some book choices for families with young children:

- A wonderful introduction to Shabbat for families with young children is the book *Shabbat Shalom!* by Michelle Shapiro Abraham, illustrated by Ann Koffsky. It tells the story of a family celebrating Shabbat and includes the prayers for lighting Shabbat candles, reciting the *Kiddush*, saying the blessing over the challah, and more. Its companion book *Shavua Tov!*, also by Michelle Shapiro Abraham, introduces the rituals that bring Shabbat to a close. Other books by Michelle Abraham that parents may find useful are *Good Morning, Boker Tov* and *Good Night, Lilah Tov*. These books are available through URJ Press. Companion CDs with songs and blessings are available for both *Shabbat Shalom!* and the *Good Morning* and *Good Night* books.
- *Come, Let Us Welcome Shabbat* by Judyth Groner and Madeline Wikler is a guide to the Friday night home observance of Shabbat, from the

dropping of coins into a *tzedakah* box to singing *Birkat HaMazon*. Songs, crafts, and a challah recipe are included. This book is available through Kar-Ben Copies, Inc.

Congregations may also want to download the "Morning Rituals and Bedtime Rituals" instructional booklets from the Union for Reform Judaism Web site (www.urj.org) to give to families. These resources are very useful for families who want to create a strong start to leading a Jewish life.

Prepare for Shabbat

The most important thing for making Shabbat special is to have special things that make the day different—apart—from other days:

- Let the week lead into Shabbat: "Only three days 'til Shabbat!" "Tomorrow is Shabbat!"
- Make one special meal each Shabbat to eat together with family and friends.
- Plan the Shabbat menu together. Make it a time for special, favorite foods. Let each family member pick a food item. Get the kids involved in the preparations: cooking, setting the table, tidying, shopping. Let each child "help" make a favorite dish, and then let her/him bring it to the table. Or give each child the choice of cutting up things like pickles.
- Have special Shabbat chores. Make a list of things that you need to do to get your home ready for Shabbat (e.g., clearing toys from the dining room table). Make a chart to show who will be responsible for each task.
- Eat sitting down together at the dining room table. Make it a festive meal, with the "good china" and flatware, a beautiful tablecloth, and real napkins! Have little inexpensive wine glasses for the kids, so they can feel special and grown-up. Have flowers on the table or a special Shabbat centerpiece.
- Have everyone help. Even the smallest child can place napkins at each place setting.
- If you are having guests, get the kids involved by having them make handmade place-setting cards.
- Let everyone join in with candlelighting and the prayers.

Encourage families to begin their celebration of Shabbat by planning something that they do not do other days of the week. Have special activities set aside for Shabbat that the family can do together. Shabbat should be different from all other days of the week. On the next page is a list of activities for making Shabbat special that you can suggest to parents and children. It is written so that you can reproduce it as is to give out after a Shabbat program or discussion.

Ideas for Making Shabbat Special at Home

Set time aside to play games, do puzzles, or watch special videos together.

Set aside special Shabbat clothes for the kids—Shabbat shoes, Shabbat hair ribbons, and so on.

Serve the kids special Shabbat-only treats.

Arrange to have your children's friends come and enjoy a Shabbat activity with them.

Wake up Shabbat morning to a table full of special food.

Keep a collection of toys and games that are exclusively for Shabbat.

Read Jewish books together.

Connect with relatives and friends. Invite them to a Shabbat meal or to do an activity with you.

Visit elderly or sick relatives and friends.

Plan to visit a retirement or nursing home weekly, if possible. Take the residents cookies you have baked or cards you have made.

Revisit Creation—take a walk outdoors and experience nature.

Use a Shabbat meal as a time for the children to show off the projects they made that week in school.

Mealtime on Shabbat gives us the perfect opportunity to discuss the questions from *Got Shabbat. Got Shabbat* is a resource from the URJ that provides information and activities for young children and their families. It can be found at http://urj.org/educate/childhood/Shabbat/.

Tell stories about your family or read books with a Jewish theme.

After Shabbat is over, when you're tucking your little ones into bed, talk about the good food and fun things you did together, then say the *Sh'ma*, a way to end every day. The *Sh'ma* can be found in Hebrew, English, and transliteration in *Good Night, Lilah Tov* (URJ Press).

Listen to Jewish music and sing Jewish songs. Here are some good CDs available from URJ Books and Music, to start with:

Shabbat Shalom! Jewish Children's Songs & Blessings for Shabbat **(CD)** Various artists. This is a good CD to listen to during Shabbat evening dinner with your family. *Shabbat Shalom!* will set the perfect mood for you, enhancing your Shabbat family experience. This collection of blessings and original songs by original artists is the companion to the URJ Press children's book of the same name. Also an excellent learning tool for blessings. Suitable for children up to age six.

Good Morning, Good Night: Jewish Children's Songs for Daytime and Bedtime **(CD)** Featuring six songs for bedtime and six for morning from contemporary Jewish music's biggest stars. A great way to start and end the day for families with young children.

My Jewish World: Kids' Songs for Everyday Living **(CD)** Judy Caplan Ginsburgh/Various artists

At-Home Crafts

You may make crafts as a part of your Tot Shabbat program. If you think families would enjoy doing so at home as well, you may wish to send some ideas home for making Shabbat ritual objects to use in their home celebrations. Creating together can be a meaningful Shabbat activity.

Following are some suggestions for easy craft ideas, made using materials families may well have at home or can get at a dollar or craft store.

Challah covers

Materials:
Handkerchief or cloth napkin
Spray bottle with water in it
Scraps of colored tissue paper
Permanent markers

Procedure:
Have children place colored tissue paper on the handkerchief or napkin. Spray water on the handkerchief. The tissue will bleed onto the handkerchief. Let it dry. It will look great. Using permanent marker, you can then add the words "Shabbat Shalom" or "Challah" or or anything else that will be meaningful to your family.

Shabbat Saltscape Candle Holders

Materials:
2 baby food jars
Small reclosable plastic bags
1 cup salt
Food coloring
Newspaper
Candles

Procedure:
Divide the salt into as many plastic bags as you want colors. Add several drops of food coloring to each bag, close tightly, and shake and knead the color into the salt. Spread each color of salt on a sheet of newspaper to air-dry. When dry, return the salt to the plastic bags. Use a spoon to sprinkle the colored salt into the jars, layering one color at a time. Carefully push one candle through the salt in each jar. The salt will keep the candle firmly upright.

Easy, Yet Beautiful *Kiddush* Cup

Materials:
Clear plastic or glass wineglass (available at dollar stores)

Press-on jewels (available at dollar or craft stores)

Pens for writing on plastic or glass (optional)

Procedure:

Make sure the glass is clean and dry. Press the jewels on the glass bowl and base in any pattern. If you wish, you can write "Shabbat" or "*Kiddush*" or any special family message on the glass with special pens from craft stores.

Tzedakah Box

Tzedakah means "justice" in Hebrew. One important understanding of *tzedakah* is helping those less fortunate than we are. It is an important part of Jewish life. Shabbat is a good time to think about how we can help others. Make a box to put money in to use for *tzedakah*.

Materials:

A small box, coffee can with plastic lid, or margarine container

Glitter, stick-on jewels, stickers, and other decorative materials

Glue

Foil

Paint

Scissors

Procedure:

Cover the can with foil, or paint it. Make a slit in the top or lid. Decorate your box with the glitter, etc. Drop a donation into the box every Friday as Shabbat begins. As a family, discuss where your money will go.

Shabbat Table Decoration

Families can make an easy, yet meaningful centerpiece for their Shabbat table using each member's handprints.

Materials:

Construction paper

Scissors

Straws or sticks

Craft dough

Glue

Pretty vase

Procedure:

Have each family member trace his or her hand on colored construction paper. Cut out the hands, and glue them to sticks or straws as stems. Put a ball of craft dough in the bottom of the vase, and stick the flower stems into the dough.

Shabbat Recipes to Send Home

Easy Challah

Use refrigerated or thawed frozen bread dough. Divide the dough into three equal pieces. Roll each piece into a long, fat, snakelike rope. Braid as you would hair. Brush with egg white, and follow package directions for rising and baking.

Make Your Own Grape Juice

You can make your own grape juice for Shabbat in a juice extractor or food processor. Go to the store together and pick out your grapes. You can use green or red grapes or mix them together. Taste each to compare flavors. Follow the directions on your juicer/processer for juice making, and have your special creation ready for your Shabbat meal.

Havdalah Activities

Havdalah is a special Jewish time. The ritual and prayers for *Havdalah* are described for young children in the book *Shavua Tov!* by Michelle Shapiro Abraham (URJ Press, 2008). After a Tot Shabbat program, send home this book or another explanation of the ritual that ends Shabbat. For some families, this simple ceremony is a meaningful way to make Shabbat special.

Following are some additional activities to suggest to families for celebrating *Havdalah*:

Create Your Own Constellations

Shabbat is officially over on Saturday night after you see at least three stars in the sky. Go or look outside together as night falls. As soon as you see stars, try to imagine the different shapes they would make if you connected them with imaginary lines. What pictures can you create? Animals? Geometric patterns? Just like astronomers, give your "constellations" names. See if you can find them again after Shabbat next week.

Guess the Scents

During the *Havdalah* service, we use a spice box to smell sweet scents to help us sweeten the coming week after Shabbat. Here's one you can make with a twist—it's also a game!

Materials:
Clean 12-cup egg carton
Paint
Scissors

6 different scented items

Procedure:

Paint or otherwise decorate the egg carton. Make holes in the top of every other egg pocket. In each of the bottom parts of the pockets with holes, put a different scent (a spice or flower or another pleasant scent). Close the box. Use it for *Havdalah*. After *Havdalah*, pass the box around and try to guess what each scent is.

Appendix C
Hebrew and Prayer Vocabulary

Tot Shabbat is an important opportunity to introduce basic prayer vocabulary. As adults we easily use words that young children may not understand. By teaching basic prayer vocabulary, we are teaching why and how we communicate with God. We are also reminding the adults in the room of some very important concepts and the reasons we are there. Below is a list of words. We should not take for granted that the children and the adults with them understand what these words and concepts mean. They can be explained as the service proceeds. This is surely not an exhaustive list, but it includes the basics. Not everything needs to be covered in one service, but be sure to reinforce what you have taught from service to service. Also, once you have gone over the words a few times, try to draw the meaning out of your participants next time. For example, if you teach them at the first Tot Shabbat of the year that "prayers" are special words we say to God, then at the next Tot Shabbat ask them what "prayers" are. This is one concept that should never be taken for granted!

Adonai: A Hebrew name for God

aron kodesh: Ark, the place where we keep the Torah.

b'rachah: Blessing, a kind of prayer that is a way of thanking God for things we have. It always starts *Baruch atah Adonai*.

challah: Bread for Shabbat.

echad: One. There is only one God.

Eloheinu: Our God.

God: We can't see, hear, smell, or touch God. But God is everywhere. We can see, hear, smell, or touch things that God made for us—like the world, our families, and us!

HaMotzi: The blessing for bread.

Israel: A special place for the Jewish people. It is far away, across the ocean. It is where the very first temple was built, long, long ago. Sometimes when we pray, we face toward Israel and the place where the first temple was.

Kiddush: The blessing over wine/juice.

kodesh: Holy, something special to God. This is a very hard concept to explain to young children.

neirot: Candles.

ner tamid: Eternal light. It is always lit to remind us that God is always around us, taking care of us. It also reminds us that we are in a holy place.

prayer: Special words we say to God. Sometimes we say these words in Hebrew, and sometimes we say them in English. Sometimes we say them together, and sometimes we say whatever is in our hearts.

Shabbat: The Sabbath, a special day. God worked hard all week making the world, and then God rested (on Shabbat). God wants us to work (play) hard all week and then rest. God also wants us to do different, special things on Shabbat that we don't do the rest of the week to make Shabbat special.

shalom: Peace. This means no fighting. God wants us to be kind and take care of each other.

Shehecheyanu: *B'rachah* we say for special occasions. Anytime we reach a holiday, special event, or milestone (birthday, first steps, first tooth) is an opportunity to say this blessing. It thanks God for keeping us alive and helping us reach a special time.

Sh'ma: Listen, hear. Pay attention. Something really important is coming (there is only one God!). The first word of the *Sh'ma* prayer.

todah: Thank you.

Torah: The scroll in the ark that is like a big book. It has special stories about the Jewish people.

tov: Good.

V'ahavta: Love. God loves us, and we love God. We love God by doing Jewish and kind things. A passage in the *Sh'ma* prayer.

Yisrael: Another name for the Jewish people.

Appendix D
Notes and Lyrics for
The Tot Shabbat Handbook CD

Editor/Producer: Cantor Alane Simons Katzew
Recording engineer: Steve Fontaine

Editorial Committee
Ellen Allard
Lisa Baydush
Carol Boyd Leon
Cantor Mia Fram Davidson
Marc Rossio
Molly Wine

Ex-officio
Steve Brodsky
Paula Feldstein
Cathy Rolland

1. BIM BAM—SHABBAT SHALOM
Music and lyrics by Nachum Frankel. Performed by Ditza Zakay, from the recording *Shabbat Shalom with Ditza*.

Bim bam, bim bim bim bam,
Bim bim bim bim bim bam (2x)

Shabbat shalom, Shabbat shalom
Shabbat, Shabbat, Shabbat, Shabbat shalom (2x)

Shabbat, Shabbat, Shabbat Shabbat shalom (2x)

Sabbath peace!

2. WE SING SHABBAT, WE SING SHALOM
Music and lyrics by Peter and Ellen Allard, ©1997 80-Z Music, Inc. Performed by Peter and Ellen Allard, www.peterandellen.com. From the recording *Sing Shalom: Songs for the Jewish Holidays*, available from URJBooksandMusic.com.

Chorus: We sing Shabbat, we sing shalom
Shabbat shalom, Shabbat shalom
We sing Shabbat, we sing shalom
Shabbat shalom, Shabbat shalom

L'hadlik ner shel Shabbat, we light the Sabbath
lights
L'hadlik ner shel Shabbat, we light the Sabbath
lights

Chorus

Borei p'ri hagafen, we drink the Sabbath wine
Borei p'ri hagafen, we drink the Sabbath wine

Chorus

Hamotzi lechem min ha-aretz, we eat the Sabbath bread
Hamotzi lechem min ha-aretz, we eat the Sabbath bread

Chorus

L'chah dodi likrat kallah, we greet the Sabbath bride
Lchah dodi likrat kallah, we greet the Sabbath bride

Chorus

3. SHABABABAT SHALOM

Music and lyrics by Craig Taubman, © 1995 Sweet Louise Music (BMI). Performed by Craig Taubman, www.craignco.com. From the recording *My Jewish Discovery*, available from URJBooksandMusic.com.

Chorus: Sha-ba-bat, Sha-ba-bat, Sha-ba-bat, Sha-ba-bat
Sha-ba-ba-ba-ba-ba-bat, Shabbat shalom
Oooeee, Shabbat shalom (2x)

Shabbat Shalom, it's the day of rest
Shabbat Shalom, it's the day I love best
Shabbat Shalom, it's the day of rest
Shabbat, Shabbat shalom

Chorus

Light the candles, say the *Kiddush* over the wine
Do the *Motzi*, the challah tastes so fine
Light the candles, say the *Kiddush* over the wine
That *Shabbos* feeling so fine

Every week I get that *Shabbos* feeling
(*Shabbos* feeling, get that *Shabbos* feeling)
I feel it from my head down to my toes
(Head down to my toes)
Six long days I have to wait for *Shabbos*
(Wait for *Shabbos*, just can't wait for *Shabbos*)
But then on Friday eve I get that *Shabbos* glow
(Get that *Shabbos* glow, Oh!)

Chorus

4. SHABBABABABAT

Music and lyrics by Sally Heckelman, ©1996 Daffodil Music. Performed by Sally and the Daffodils, www.sallyandthedaffodils.com. From the recording *Tap Your Feet to a Jewish Beat*.

Chorus: Shabba-ba-ba-bat, Shabbat shalom (doo, doo, doo, doo)
Shabba-ba-ba-bat, Shabbat shalom (doo, doo, doo, doo)
Shabba-ba-ba-bat, Shabbat shalom (doo, doo, doo, doo)
Shabbat, Shabbat shalom

We light the candles every Friday night (Shabbat shalom) (3x)
Shabbat, Shabbat shalom

Chorus

We say the *Kiddush* every Friday night (Shabbat shalom) (3x)
Shabbat, Shabbat shalom

Chorus

We eat the challah and it tastes so good (Yummy!) (3x)
Shabbat, Shabbat shalom

Chorus

5. SHAKE ANOTHER HAND

Folk song, lyrics adapted by Sue Epstein. Performed by Cantor Marcelo Gindlin, www.mjcs.org. From the recording *Shabbat and Holidays with Cantor Marcelo and Friends*.

Sha-ba-ba-ba, Shabbat shalom, Shabbat shalom
Sha-ba-ba-ba, Shabbat, Shabbat shalom

Shake another hand, shake a hand next to you
Shake another hand Shabbat shalom
Shake another hand, shake a hand next to you
Shake another hand and say, Shabbat shalom
(Everybody now)

Chorus: La la la la la . . .
Shabbat shalom

Scratch another back, scratch a back next to you
Scratch another back Shabbat shalom
Scratch another back, scratch a back next to you
Scratch another back and say, Shabbat shalom
(Everybody now)

Chorus

Tickle another belly, tickle a belly next to you
Tickle another belly Shabbat shalom
Tickle another belly, tickle a belly next to you
Tickle another belly and say, Shabbat shalom
(Everybody now)

Chorus

Give another hug, give a hug next to you
Give another hug Shabbat Shalom
Give another hug, give a hug next to you
Give another hug and say, Shabbat Shalom

Chorus

6. CANDLE BLESSING

Music by A. W. Binder, text from liturgy. Performed by Cantor Angela Warnick Buchdahl, from the recording *Shabbat Music at WRT.*

Baruch atah Adonai, Eloheinu Melech haolam,
Asher kid'shanu b'mitzvotav, v'tzivanu,
L'hadlik ner, l'hadlik ner shel Shabbat.

Blessed are You, Adonai our God, Sovereign of the universe, who hallows us with mitzvot, commanding us to kindle the light of Shabbat.

7. L'CHAH DODI

Music by Mordechai Zeira, text by Shlomo Alkabetz (16th century). Performed by children's choruses in New York and New Jersey. From the recording *Shiron L'Yeladim: Songs for Children ages 6–9,* available from URJBooksandMusic.com.

L'chah dodi likrat kalah, likrat kalah
P'nei Shabbat n'kab'lah, n'kablah. (2x)

Shabbat shalom, Shabbat shalom, Shabbat shalom
um'vorach. (2x)

Beloved, come to meet the bride; beloved come to
     greet Shabbat.
Sabbath peace and blessings.

8. BOKER TOV

Music and lyrics by Marc Rossio, a.k.a. The Marvelous Toy; © 2005 The Marvelous Toy, LLC (ASCAP). Performed by Marc Rossio, www.themarveloustoy.com. From the recording *L'Chaim—To Life!,* available from URJBooksandMusic.com.

Chorus: *Boker, boker tov, boker or lachem* (2x)

Good morning to you!
The sun's risen too.
Let a smile light up your face.
Put your feet on the floor, and march them right
     out the door.
Giddy up, giddy out, giddy go, and start the day.

Chorus

In the morning I greet,
all the people I meet,
with a *boker tov* in a friendly way.
I'm excited to see that my friends are here with
     me.
Giddy up, giddy out, giddy go, and start the day.

Chorus

9. TOTS' MODEH ANI

Music and lyrics by Carol Boyd Leon, ©2006 Carol Boyd Leon (ASCAP), www.carolboydleon.com. Performed by the Hannah Senesh Community Day School Chorus, conducted by Chana Rothman.

Modeh ani l'fanecha,
Thank you God is what I want to say.
Modeh ani l'fanecha,
Thank you God for this wonderful day!

Modah ani l'fanecha,
Thank you God is what I want to say.
Modah ani l'fanecha,
Thank you God for this wonderful day!

10. BAR'CHU

Music by Benjamin Siegel, text from liturgy. Performed by Cantor Rachel Stock Spilker with the Shir Chants, Shir Tzion, and Torah Tones choirs of Mt. Zion Temple, St. Paul, MN. From the recording *Shirei Tzion, Songs of Zion.*

La, la, la, la . . .
Bar'chu et Adonai ham'vorach!
Baruch Adonai ham'vorach, ham'vorach l'olam
va-ed.

Praise Adonai to whom praise is due forever!
Praised be Adonai to whom praise is due, now and
     forever!

11. BAR'CHU

Music by Carol Boyd Leon, text from liturgy; © 2000 Carol Boyd Leon (ASCAP). Performed by Carol Boyd Leon, www.carolboydleon.com. From the recording *Songs from the Heart: Family Shabbat*, available from URJBooksandMusic.com.

La, la, la, la
Bar'chu et Adonai ham'vorach!
Baruch Adonai ham'vorach l'olam va-ed! (2x)

Praise Adonai to whom praise is due forever!
Praised be Adonai to whom praise is due, now and
   forever!

12. SH'MA

Music by Solomon Sulzer, text from Deuteronomy 6:4 and liturgy. Performed by Madeleine Manasse.

Sh'ma Yisrael, Adonai Eloheinu, Adonai Echad!
Baruch shem k'vod malchuto l'olam va-ed.

Hear, O Israel, Adonai is our God, Adonai is One!
Blessed is God's glorious majesty forever and ever.

13. SH'MA

Music by Tzvika Pik, text from Deuteronomy 6:4 and liturgy; ©ACUM, Ltd. Performed by Daniel Leanse, from the recording *Congregation Micah: Music at Micah*, www.congregationmicah.org.

Sh'ma Yisrael, Adonai Eloheinu, Adonai Echad!
   (4x)
Baruch shem k'vod, shem k'vod malchuto l'olam va-
   ed. (2x)
Sh'ma Yisrael, Adonai Eloheinu, Adonai Echad!
   (2x)

Hear, O Israel, Adonai is our God, Adonai is One!
Blessed is God's glorious majesty forever and ever.

14. THE CHILDREN'S SH'MA

Music and lyrics by Carol Boyd Leon, Hebrew text from Deuteronomy 6:4 and liturgy; © 2000 Carol Boyd Leon (ASCAP). Performed by Carol Boyd Leon and the "Chai Notes" Youth Chorus, www.carolboydleon.com. From the recording *Songs from the Heart: Family Shabbat*, available from URJBooksandMusic.com.

Sh'ma Yisrael, listen everyone,
Adonai Eloheinu, Adonai our God is one.
Adonai Echad
We sing it loud and clear
Adonai Echad
We sing for all to hear
Baruch shem k'vod malchuto l'olam va-ed
We praise God's name each and every day,
Forever and ever and that is why we say,
Sh'ma Yisrael, listen everyone,
Adonai Eloheinu, Adonai our God is One,
Adonai our God is One. ♪

15. GOD IS EVERYWHERE

Music and lyrics by Peter and Ellen Allard, © 1988 80-Z Music, Inc. Performed by Peter & Ellen Allard, www.peterandellen.com. Previously unreleased.

Chorus: God is everywhere and God is One, God
            is One
         God is everywhere and God is One, God
            is One
         God is everywhere and God is One
         In the moon, in the stars, in the shining
            sun,
         God is everywhere and God is One, God
            is One

In my eyes, God is One
In my hands, God is One
In my mouth, God is One
And in my feet, God is One

Chorus

In the trees, God is One
In the sky, God is One
In the flowers, God is One
And in the water, God is One

Chorus

In my friends, God is One
In my family, God is One
In my neighbors, God is One
And in my world, God is One

Chorus

16. V'AHAVTA

Cantillation. Performed by Madeleine Manasse.

V'ahavta et Adonai Elohecha
B'chol l'vav'cha, uv'chol nafsh'cha, uv'chol
  m'odecha.
V'hayu had'varim ha-eileh
Asher anochi m'tzavcha hayom al l'vavecha.

You shall love Adonai your God with all your
  heart,
With all your soul, and with all your might.
Take to heart these instructions with which I charge
  you this day.

17. V'SHINANTAM L'VANECHA

Author unknown. Performed by the Hannah Senesh
Community Day School Chorus (Brooklyn, NY),
conducted by Chana Rothman.

V'shinantam l'vanecha v'dibarta bam,
V'dibarta bam, v'dibarta bam ba-dam ba-bam
V'shinantam l'vanecha v'dibarta bam,
V'dibarta bam, v'dibarta bam bam, bam ba-dam ba-
  bam

B'shivt'cha b'veitecha,
Uv'lecht'cha vaderech,
Uv'shochb'cha, uv'kumecha,
V'dibarta bam ba-dam ba-bam. (2x)

Bam ba-dam bam-bam
bam ba-dam ba-bam
v'dibarta bam ba-dam ba-bam (2x)

Impress them upon your children.
Recite them when you stay at home and when you
  are away,
When you lie down and when you get up.

18. LOVE *ADONAI*

Music by Robbi Sherwin, text from Deuteronomy
6:5–9; © 2007 by Sababa. Performed by Sababa,
www.sababamusic.com. From the recording *Pray
for the Peace*, available from URJBooksandMusic.
com.

Chorus: Love *Adonai* your God (4x)

With all your heart
With all your soul
With all your might. (2x)

Chorus

Take these words
That I command this day
And keep them in your heart. (2x)

Chorus

Write them on the doorposts of your house, and on
  your gates (2x)

Chorus

19. MI CHAMOCHA

Music by Debbie Friedman, text from Exodus 15:11,
18; © 1988/1989 Deborah Lynn Friedman (ASCAP).
Performed by Debbie Friedman, www.debbiefried-
man.com. From the recording *And You Shall Be a
Blessing*, available from URJBooksandMusic.com.

Yai lai lai lai…

Mi chamochah ba-eilim, Adonai!
Mi kamochah nedar bakodesh,
Nora t'hilot oseh fele,
Nora t'hilot oseh fele!

Malchut'cha ra-u vanecha,
Bokei-a yam lifnei Moshe (uMiryam).
Zeh Eli, anu v'amru,
Zeh Eli, anu v'amru!

Adonai yimloch l'olam va-ed!
Adonai yimloch l'olam va-ed!

Mi chamochah ba-eilim Adonai!
Mi kamochah nedar bakodesh,
Nora t'hilot oseh fele,
Nora t'hilot oseh fele!

Yai lai lai lai…

Who is like You, O God, among the gods that are
  worshipped?
Who is like You, majestic in holiness, awesome in
  splendor, doing wonders?
Your children witnessed your sovereignty, the sea
  splitting before Moses (and Miriam).
"This is our God!" they cried. "Adonai will reign
  forever and ever."

20. STANDING AT THE SEA

Music and lyrics by Peter and Ellen Allard, © 2003 80-Z Music, Inc. Performed by Peter and Ellen Allard, www.peterandellen.com. From the recording *Bring the Sabbath Home*, available from URJBooksandMusic.com.

Standing at the sea, *mi chamochah* (3x)
Freedom's on our way.
Singing and dancing, *mi chamochah* (3x)
Freedom's on our way.

Chorus: Freedom, freedom (3x)
              Freedom's on our way.

They're coming up behind, *mi chamochah* (3x)
Freedom's on our way.
Bound no more, *mi chamocha*h (3x)
Freedom's on our way.

Chorus

The sea she parts, *mi chamochah* (3x)
Freedom's on our way.
Walking through the water, *mi chamochah* (3x)
Freedom's on our way.

Chorus

We're on the other side, *mi chamochah* (3x)
Freedom's on our way.
One God, *mi chamochah* (3x)
Freedom's on our way.

Chorus

21. ACROSS THE SEA

Music and lyrics by Carol Boyd Leon, © 2009 Carol Boyd Leon (ASCAP). Performed by Carol Boyd Leon, www.carolboydleon.com. From the recording *Dayenu! A Passover Haggadah for Families and Children.*

Come with me into the water.
Come with me across the sea.
Israel's sons and Israel's daughters
Come with me, we're going to be free

Forward, forward to our freedom
Forward, forward through the sea
Watch the water open for us
God's own hand will set us free

Mi chamochah ba-eilim Adonai?
Who is like You *Adonai?*
There is none like You, our God,
Who opened up the sea and helped us to be free.

22. HOLY HOLINESS

Music and lyrics by Peter and Ellen Allard, © 2003 80-Z Music, Inc. Performed by Peter and Ellen Allard, www.peterandellen.com. From the recording *Bring the Sabbath Home*, available from URJBooksandMusic.com.

All around
Everywhere
All around, everywhere
Holy, holiness.

In the highest sky
In the deepest sea
In the highest sky, in the deepest sea
Holy, holiness.

In my heart
In your soul
In my heart, in your soul
Holy, holiness.

In all we do
In all we are
In all we do, in all we are
Holy, holiness.

Every step
Every breath
Every step, every breath
Holy, holiness.

As with me
So with you
As with me, so with you
Holy, holiness.

All around
Everywhere
All around, everywhere
Holy, holiness.

23. I'M PRAYING

Music and lyrics by Rabbi Neil Comess-Daniels, © 2008 Neil Comess-Daniels. Performed by Rabbi Neil Comess-Daniels, www.bethshirsholom.org. Previously unreleased.

I'm swaying, I guess I'm praying
Listening to the feelings deep inside
I'm bending, I guess I'm sending
Thoughts I usually carry in my mind

Chorus: Who do you think is listening to me?
           Do you think there's anyone there?
           I know that I am listening to me
           And I know that I care
           It doesn't matter if I say the words right
           Sometimes they come out all wrong
           It doesn't matter if I know the melody
           Sometimes I sing my own song

I'm being, I guess I'm seeing
Everything I do and all that I say
I'm knowing, I guess I'm growing
Everything I am in every way

Chorus

I'm swaying, I guess I'm praying
Listening to the feelings deep inside

24. THANK YOU GOD
Music and lyrics by Doug Cotler and Jeff Marks, ©
2009 Wail and Blubber Music (BMI). Performed by
Doug Cotler in a newly updated recording, www.
dougcotler.com. Original version from the recording
It's So Amazing!, available from URJBooksandMusic.
com.

Chorus: *Baruch Atah Adonai*, thank You God
           Baruch Atah Adonai, thank You God

Thank you for the candles
Thank you for the wine
Thank you for the challah
That always tastes so fine

Chorus

Thank you for the people
Who always care for me
They love me and they help me
We're a family

Chorus

Thank you for my friends
And thank you for my toys
Thank you God for watching over
All the girls and boys

Chorus

25. SIM SHALOM
Folk song. Performed by Orit Perlman, www.oritper-
lman.com. From the recording *Tfilotai*.

Sim, sim, sim shalom
Sim, sim, sim shalom
Sim, sim, sim shalom
Tovah uv'rachah

Lai lai lai…

Grant peace, goodness, and blessing

26. MY SILENT PRAYER
Music and lyrics by Marc Rossio, a.k.a. The Marvelous Toy, © 2005 The Marvelous Toy, LLC. Performed by Marc Rossio, www.themarveloustoy.com.
From the recording *L'Chaim—To Life*, available
from URJBooksandMusic.com.

This is the moment as time rolls by
For my silent prayer to *Adonai*

Chorus: A prayer of thanks for all my blessings
           A prayer of compassion for all in need
           A prayer of knowledge, for I keep
              guessing
           A prayer between God and me

Close your eyes, say a prayer
Adonai will be there

Chorus

27. OSEH SHALOM
Music by Nurit Hirsch, text from liturgy; © ACUM,
Ltd. Performed by children's choruses in New
York and New Jersey. From the recording *Shiron
L'Yeladim: Songs for Children ages 6–9*, available
from URJBooksandMusic.com.

Oseh shalom bimromav
Hu yaaseh shalom aleinu
V'al kol Yisrael
V'imru, v'imru, Amen.

Yaaseh shalom, yaaseh shalom
Shalom Aleinu v'al kol Yisrael (4x)

May the One who makes peace in the high heavens
     make peace for us and for all Israel. Amen.

28. YIH'YU
Music by Dan Nichols, text from Psalm 19:15; © 2002 Eighteen Entertainment. Performed by Dan Nichols and E18hteen, www.jewishrock.com. From the recording *Kol HaShabbat*, available from URJBooksandMusic.com.

Yih'yu (Yih'yu) l'ratzon (l'ratzon) imrei fi
V'hegyon libi l'fanecha
Adonai (Adonai) tzuri (tzuri) v'go-ali
Adonai tzuri v'go-ali

May the words of my mouth
And the meditations of my heart
Be acceptable to You, oh God
My Rock and my Redeemer

29. TREE OF LIFE
Music by Richard Silverman, text from Proverbs 3:18. Performed by Cantor Richard Silverman.

Chorus: Shalom, shalom (4x)

Eitz chayim hi lamachazikim bah
V'tom'cheha m'ushar (2x)

Chorus

It is a tree of life to them that hold fast to it
And all its supporters are happy (2x)

Chorus

D'rachehah darchei no-am
V'chol n'tivoteha shalom (2x)

Its ways are ways of pleasantness
And all its paths are peace
Its ways are ways of pleasantness
And all its paths are shalom

Chorus

30. TORAH TORAH
Folk song. Performed by Cindy Paley, www.cindypaley.com. From the recording *Celebrate with Cindy* —available from URJBooksandMusic.com.

Torah Torah Torah,
Torah Torah Torah,
Torah tzivah lanu Moshe. (2x)

Torah Torah,
Torah Torah,
Torah tzivah lanu Moshe. (2x)

Moses commanded us the Torah

31. HAKAFA
Music and lyrics by Peter and Ellen Allard, © 2001 80-Z Music, Inc. Performed by Peter and Ellen Allard, www.peterandellen.com. Previously unreleased.

Chorus: *Hakafah* we go around, and around, and around, and around, and
Hakafah we go around, and around, and around (2x)

We're marching with the Torah we love, love, love, love, love.
We're marching with the Torah, given by God above.
Yes, God is up, and down, and in, and out, and all around!

Chorus

(For additional verses, substitute different words for "marching," e.g., dancing, tiptoeing, skipping.)

32. BUILDING A BETTER WORLD
Music and lyrics by Peter and Ellen Allard, © 2002 80-Z Music, Inc. Performed by Peter and Ellen Allard featuring vocalist Eric Webster, www.peterandellen.com. From the recording *Sing It! Say It! Stamp It! Sway It!* Volume 3.

We're building a better world, we're building a better world
We're building a better world, one person at a time.

Chorus: And the world goes round and round
The world goes round and round and round
And the world goes round and round
The world goes round and round and round

We're building a world with love, we're building a world with love
We're building a world with love, one person at a time

Chorus

We're building a world with peace, we're building a world with peace
We're building a world with peace, one person at a time

Chorus

We're building a world with friends, we're building
a world with friends
We're building a world with friends, one person at
a time

Chorus

33. A BLESSING FOR THE ONES YOU LOVE

Music and lyrics by Debbie Friedman, © 1994. Performed by Debbie Friedman, www.debbiefriedman.com. From the recording *Shirim Al Galgalim*.

May God bless you and keep you
Every moment every day
May God smile at you
And fill your heart in every way
May God help you find the goodness
In everything you do
May you be blessed with peace from above

Y'simeich Elohim k'Sarah, Rivkah, Rachel, v'Leah.
Y'simcha Elohim k'Efrayim v'chiM'nasheh.
Y'varech'cha Adonai v'yishm'recha.
Ya-eir Adonai panav eilecha vichuneka.
Yisa Adonai panav eilecha v'yaseim l'cha shalom.

May God inspire you to live like Sarah, Rebecca,
Rachel, and Leah;
God inspire you to live like Ephraim and
Menasseh.
May God bless you and keep you. May God's light
shine upon you, and may God be gracious to
you. May you feel God's Presence within you
always, and may you find peace.

34. BLESSING FOR SHALOM

Music and lyrics by Jeff Klepper, © 2009 Jeff Klepper. Performed by Cantor Jeff Klepper (www.jeffklepper.com) and Ellen Allard (www.peterandellen.com). Previously unreleased.

Y'varech'cha Adonai v'yishm'recha
Ya-eir Adonai panav eilecha vichuneka
Yisah Adonai panav eilecha v'yaseim l'cha shalom

It's a blessing for you, it's a blessing for me
A blessing for each member of our family
A blessing for everyone here in our home
A blessing for shalom (2x)

May God bless you and keep you
And fill you with light
May God send you courage to do what is right
May God's face shine upon you with kindness and
love
And bless you with peace from above.

35. BOREI P'RI HAGAFEN (Blessing for Wine/ Grape Juice)

Text from liturgy. Performed by Madeleine Manasse.

Baruch atah, Adonai Eloheinu, Melech haolam,
borei p'ri hagafen

Praise to You, Adonai our God, Sovereign of the
universe, Creator of the fruit of the vine.

36. HAMOTZI (Blessing for Bread)

Text from liturgy. Performed by Madeleine Manasse.

Baruch atah, Adonai Eloheinu, Melech haolam,
hamotzi lechem min haaretz

Praise to You, Adonai our God, Sovereign of the universe, who brings forth bread from the earth.

37. SHALOM ALEICHEM, PEACE TO US

Music lyrics by Carol Boyd Leon; © 2006 Carol Boyd Leon (ASCAP). Performed by Carol Boyd Leon, www.carolboydleon.com. From the recording *Gan Shirim: A Garden of Songs*—available from URJBooksandMusic.com.

Shalom aleichem, peace to you
Shalom aleichem, peace to us (2x)

We have come together here in peace
May our going also be in peace (2x)

38. KI ESHMERA SHABBAT/IF I TAKE GOOD CARE OF SHABBAT

Baghdad Folk melody, text by Abraham Ibn Ezra. Performed by Sue Epstein. From the recording, *NU!?!? From Sue: Fun Jewish Songs Little Kids Love to Sing*—available from URJBooksandMusic.com.

If I take good care of Shabbat, God will take care of me
If I take good care of Shabbat, God will take care of me

It's a sign forever between us, all through history
It's a sign forever between us, between God and me

Ki eshm'rah Shabbat Eil yishm'reini
Ki eshm'rah Shabbat Eil yishm'reini

Ot hi l'olmei ad beino u'veini
Ot hi l'olmei ad beino u'veini

Shabbat shalom, Shabbat shalom
Shabbat Shabbat Shabbat Shabbat shalom. (2x)

I love you *Shabbat kodesh*, you are my day of rest
I'll dress up in my nicest clothes and greet you as my guest
Oh, *Shabbat kodesh* how I wait for you
Each and every night, the whole week through.

39. ENDLESS POSSIBILITIES (for *Havdalah*)

Music and lyrics by Todd Herzog, © 2009 Todd Herzog/Dared Knot Music, LLC. Performed by Todd Herzog, www.toddherzog.com. Previously unreleased. From the 2009 Conference of Early Childhood Educators of Reform Judaism.

Take a deep breath we'll take time to remember
Close our eyes and put the past behind
We'll gather together, it's the end and the beginning
The sweet smell will bring us there
With endless possibilities in the air

We pass the silver box from generation to generation
The twisted candle flickers, light dancing in our eyes
We raise the *Kiddush* cup, the flame sizzles in the wine
Our arms around each other as another week arrives
So take a deep breath...

Contributors

Peter and Ellen Allard are multiaward-winning recording artists, composers, and early childhood music specialists. They present family concerts, Tot and Family Shabbat worship services, keynote presentations, and teacher workshops throughout the United States, Canada, and Europe. The Allards have released eight CDs and five songbooks. Their compositions have been recorded by other well-known children's performers and recording artists and are used in many synagogues and religious schools. They have been on the faculty of the North American Jewish Choral Festival and Hava Nashira (the annual URJ song leaders' training) and have presented workshops, performed concerts, and led family services at the URJ Biennial and CAJE. Peter Allard is a graduate of Worcester State College, with a bachelor's degree in health education. Ellen Allard is a graduate of Boston University, with a bachelor's degree in music. She earned her master's degree in early childhood education at Arcadia University.

Lorraine Posner Arcus is nationally recognized for her work in the fields of early childhood Judaic curriculum and Israeli dance for children and teens. She is a veteran teacher of kindergarten Judaica at the Bet Shraga Hebrew Academy in Albany, New York. Her book *Torah Alive!*, published by URJ Press, is reflective of her innovative and original curriculum. As director of Israeli Dance at Temple Israel in Albany, she is artistic director of Tzamarot, a teen performing group. She is the author of *Zman Lirkod: A Manual for Teaching Israeli Dance*. She conducts annual Israeli dance leadership training programs for teens and adults, locally and nationally. Arcus is a recipient of the 2001 Covenant Award for Outstanding Creative Jewish Educators.

Nancy Bossov, RJE, is the director of early childhood education at the Board of Jewish Education of Greater New York. She is very involved in national organizations advocating for excellence in Jewish early childhood education, including the National Association of Jewish Early Childhood Specialists, the Alliance for Early Education, and Early Childhood Educators of Reform Judaism. She is also passionate about Jewish music and teaches teens to play guitar and songlead. She received her BS in music therapy from New York University, MA in music education from Teachers College–Columbia University, and MA in religious education from Hebrew Union College–Jewish Institute of Religion.

Rabbi Deborah Bravo is currently serving as the rabbi at Temple Emanu-El in Edison, New Jersey. She has been the synagogue's spiritual leader since July 2006, when she came there from Congregation B'nai Jeshurun in Short Hills, New Jersey. Ordained in 1998 by Hebrew Union College–Jewish Institute of Religion in Cincinnati, Rabbi Bravo also holds a master's in education from Xavier University. Her passions range from teaching to music to children, and she enjoys being involved with the larger community, both Jewish and interfaith. She and her husband David reside in Maplewood, New Jersey with their two children, Samuel and Sophie.

Rabbi Shawna Brynjegard-Bialik was ordained by Hebrew Union College–Jewish Institute of Religion in 2002. She lives in California with her artist husband and three daughters, where her rabbinate is focused on life-cycle rituals and camp liturgy. She has been active on the Temple Ahavat Shalom Tot Shabbat committee for the past seven years and is currently at work on a children's book with her sister.

Treasure L. Cohen is a Jewish family educator who served as director of family and community education at the Jewish Education Association of MetroWest (New Jersey) for many years. Thirty years ago, as a young parent, she and her husband Rich developed Shabbat and holiday services for young children and their families at Congregation Beth El in South Orange, New Jersey, and she continues to lead services and train other leaders today. She has presented workshops throughout the country on Tot Shabbat as well as on Jewish early childhood and family education and has published a number of articles on these topics. She is currently a student at the Davidson Graduate School of Education at the Jewish Theological Seminary, a professor of child development at Montclair State University, a Jewish education consultant, and a storyteller.

Rabbi Paula Feldstein was ordained by Hebrew Union College–Jewish Institute of Religion in 1993. Rabbi Feldstein has served as a congregational rabbi at North Shore Congregation Israel, in Glencoe, Illinois, and at Temple Emanuel in Worcester, Massachusetts. She has also filled many other roles at those congregations, including family educator, retreat director, URJ camp faculty member, and high school director. In 2001 she became the first Reform rabbi to serve as a director of early childhood education, at Temple Emanuel in Worcester, Massachusetts. She is currently the coordinator for "Shalom Baby" at the UJA Federation of Northern New Jersey and the editor of this book.

Rabbi Elyse D. Frishman was ordained in 1981 by Hebrew Union College–Jewish Institute of Religion. Rabbi Frishman is the spiritual leader of Congregation B'nai Jeshurun, The Barnert Temple in Franklin Lakes, New Jersey. Rabbi Frishman is nationally recognized as a leader in transforming Reform Jewish worship and as a writer and editor of liturgy. She served on the UAHC-CCAR Joint Commission on Religious Living and the CCAR Liturgy Committee, the Hebrew Union College Board of Alumni Overseers, and the board of the CCAR. She served as a faculty fellow for Synagogue 2000, a national, transdenominational project transforming the culture of the synagogue from a corporate to spiritual center. In 2007, Rabbi Frishman was recognized as the second most influential American Jew in the *Forward's* "Top Fifty Jews," for editing the pioneering new Reform prayer book, *Mishkan T'filah*, published in October 2007.

Roberta Louis Goodman, EdD, RJE, is the director of research and standards for the Jewish Early Childhood Education Initiative and adjunct associate professor of Jewish education, Siegal College of Judaic Studies. She received a master's degree in Jewish education from the Rhea Hirsch School of Education at HUC-JIR. She is a past president of NATE. Goodman's publications include curricula, student materials, and articles in the areas of faith development and spirituality, research and evaluation, adult education, Jewish educational personnel, grant writing, and other topics. Recently she received the 2008 National Jewish Book Award in Jewish Education and Identity along with her co-editors for *What We NOW Know about Jewish Education*, which presents research and evaluation in the field.

Eva Grayzel is a performance artist specializing in Jewish folklore. Her uniquely interactive performances have brought her to the 92nd Street Y, the Jewish Arts Festival of Houston, Temple Emanuel of Honolulu, the Jewish Museum in New York, the Israel Independence Day Parade in Philadelphia, and the Allentown Symphony Orchestra's Children's Series. Her award-winning recordings and videos include *A Story a Day* and *The Secret in Bubbe's Attic*. Grayzel offers educator workshops on interactive storytelling techniques, parent workshops on adding meaning to Jewish rituals, and even a "trope aerobics" class.

Rachel Kamin is the director of the Joseph and Mae Gray Cultural & Learning Center at North Suburban Synagogue Beth El in Highland Park, Illinois. Prior to that, she worked as the preschool liaison librarian at the Des Plaines Public Library in Des Plaines, Illinois, and as the director of the Libraries & Media Center at Temple Israel in West Bloomfield, Michigan. She has served as chair of the Sydney Taylor Book Award Committee, a national committee of the Association of Jewish Libraries that presents awards to the best Jewish children's books each year, and frequently gives presentations and workshops about Jewish children's literature at education and library conferences around the country. She has authored articles for *BookLinks*, *Jewish Book World*, and *Judaica Librarianship* and also writes children's book reviews for *School Library Journal*, *Jewish Book World*, and the *Newsletter of the Association of Jewish Libraries*. Kamin holds a BA in history from Grinnell College and a master's degree in library and information science from the University of Michigan.

Cantor Alane Simons Katzew, worship and music specialist at the Union for Reform Judaism, is editor of *Divrei Shir*, an adult education curriculum that chronicles the development of music in the Reform Synagogue from the 1800s through the modern day. Cantor Katzew is an editorial consultant for Transcontinental Music Publications and a featured recording artist on the CDs *Shabbat Anthology* and *Nigun Anthology*. She recently engineered the complete MP3 recordings for all fifty-four weekly Torah and Haftarah portions, now available at URJBooksandMusic.com. She has previously served congregations in Ohio, Illinois, and New York. She was a cantor and faculty member at HUC-JIR in Jerusalem, thereby becoming the first invested woman cantor to function in the state of Israel. Cantor Katzew has served as both an officer and board member of the American Conference of Cantors (ACC) and on the Union for Reform Judaism commissions on Social Action and Religious Living.

Carol Boyd Leon is known for her easy-to-sing, memorable melodies and the music fun she brings to her students as an early childhood music specialist in the Washington metropolitan area, where she leads Shabbat services for tots through retirees, directs choirs, and teaches music at several preschools and religious schools. A prolific and award-winning composer, she has written an extensive collection of Jewish songs for children as well as liturgical songs for adults. Her songbooks and recordings include *Gan Shirim, A Garden of Songs*; *Songs from the Heart—Family Shabbat*; *Dayenu! A Passover Haggadah for Families and Children*; *Voices in Prayer*; *Jewish Life Cycle*; and *A Healing Service in Song* (DVD).

Rabbi Jordan Millstein was ordained by Hebrew Union College–Jewish Institute of Religion in 1993. Rabbi Millstein served as an assistant and associate rabbi at North Shore Congregation Israel in Glencoe, Illinois, from 1993 to 1999. He served as the rabbi at Temple Emanuel in Worcester, Massachusetts, from 1999 to 2008, and he currently serves Temple Sinai in Tenafly, New Jersey.

Diane G. Person, PhD, is the co-author of *Stories of Heaven and Earth: Bible Heroes in Contemporary Children's Literature*, co-editor of *The Encyclopedia of Children's Literature*, and author of several other books on using children's literature in the classroom. A children's librarian, she teaches children's literature and reading courses at Long Island University in Brooklyn, New York, and served on the Newbery Award committee.

Marilyn Price is a professional puppeteer, storyteller, and educator. She travels from coast to coast and enjoys challenges of all kinds. Her wide assortment of venues ranges from Ellis Island to libraries and schools and faith communities with a specialty in Judaica. A veteran of over thirty-five years in the business of telling and listening, she lives in Evanston, Illinois. Visit her there or more conveniently at www.marilynprice.com.

Rabbi Sue Ann Wasserman was the director of the Union for Reform Judaism's Department of Worship, Music and Religious Living from 1997 to 2009. Before joining the staff of the URJ, she was the associate rabbi at The Temple in Atlanta, Georgia (1987–1991), and the rabbi of Brooklyn Heights Synagogue in Brooklyn, New York (1991–1997). Rabbi Wasserman received her rabbinic ordination from Hebrew Union College–Jewish Institute of Religion, New York, in 1987. Four translated poems from her rabbinic thesis, *Women's Voices: Our Present Through Our Past* (a study of modern Hebrew poetry about biblical women, written by women poets), and "*Mikvah* Ceremony for Laura" (a ceremony for survivors of rape) were published in *Four Centuries of Jewish Women's Spirituality*, edited by Ellen Umansky and Dianne Ashton (Boston: Beacon Press, 1992).

Kitty Wolf holds an MA in early childhood education, an MA in art education, and a BA in Jewish history. She serves as the educator at Temple Sinai,

Portsmouth, Virginia, and the principal of a supplementary religious school that serves the children from both Conservative and Reform congregations. She worked for twenty years as director of the USDA Child and Adult Care Food Program for a nonprofit agency serving Maryland, Virginia, and the District of Columbia. She worked on task forces that developed and implemented child-care standards for the state of Virginia and the U.S. Navy. She has been an adjunct faculty member of Virginia Commonwealth University and Tidewater Community College, where she developed and taught early childhood management and teacher training courses.